THE
PRESIDENTIAL
CAMPAIGN

☆ ☆ ☆ ☆ ☆ ☆ ☆ ☆ ☆ ☆ ☆ ☆ ☆ ☆ ☆

An essay by STEPHEN HESS

Third Edition

THE BROOKINGS INSTITUTION
Washington, D.C.

Copyright © 1988 by
THE BROOKINGS INSTITUTION
1775 Massachusetts Avenue, N.W., Washington, D.C. 20036

Library of Congress Cataloging-in-Publication Data
Hess, Stephen.
  The Presidential campaign.
  Bibliography: p.
  Includes index.
  1. Presidents—United States—Election. 1. Title.
JK528.H45 1988   324.973   87-27858
ISBN 0-8157-3600-2
ISBN 0-8157-3599-5 (pbk.)

9 8 7 6 5 4 3

THE BROOKINGS INSTITUTION is an independent organization devoted to nonpartisan research, education, and publication in economics, government, foreign policy, and the social sciences generally. Its principal purposes are to aid in the development of sound public policies and to promote public understanding of issues of national importance.

The Institution was founded on December 8, 1927, to merge the activities of the Institute for Government Research, founded in 1916, the Institute of Economics, founded in 1922, and the Robert Brookings Graduate School of Economics and Government, founded in 1924.

The Board of Trustees is responsible for the general administration of the Institution, while the immediate direction of the policies, program, and staff is vested in the President, assisted by an advisory committee of the officers and staff. The by-laws of the Institution state: "It is the function of the Trustees to make possible the conduct of scientific research, and publication, under the most favorable conditions, and to safeguard the independence of the research staff in the pursuit of their studies and in the publication of the results of such studies. It is not a part of their function to determine, control, or influence the conduct of particular investigations or the conclusions reached."

The President bears final responsibility for the decision to publish a manuscript as a Brookings book. In reaching his judgment on the competence, accuracy, and objectivity of each study, the President is advised by the director of the appropriate research program and weighs the views of a panel of expert outside readers who report to him in confidence on the quality of the work. Publication of a work signifies that it is deemed a competent treatment worthy of public consideration but does not imply endorsement of conclusions or recommendations.

The Institution maintains its position of neutrality on issues of public policy in order to safeguard the intellectual freedom of the staff. Hence interpretations or conclusions in Brookings publications should be understood to be solely those of the authors and should not be attributed to the Institution, to its trustees, officers, or other staff members, or to the organizations that support its research.

For Carole and Morty

Foreword

THE WAY presidents are chosen has come under intense attack in the past decade or more. Critics have maintained that campaigns are too long and too expensive, that the issues are given too little coverage and the contenders' personalities too much, especially by network television, from which the electorate receives most of its information. There have also been serious concerns about the qualifications and characters of the candidates, and whether the election system as it is currently set up encourages the best candidates to run.

Given these criticisms, and as Americans turn their attention to electing a new chief executive, it is especially appropriate for Brookings to publish the third edition of this book. In this essay Stephen Hess examines the campaign process—the way it works, the influences upon it, the way it influences the selection of candidates. His conclusions are sobering: unlike most political scientists and political journalists, Hess believes that change in the selection system will not fundamentally change the results, that regardless of the different schemes that have been proposed for choosing presidential candidates, the process will come up with essentially the same type of person as in the past. If he is correct, it could be argued that the best way ultimately to improve the quality of our presidents would be through better methods of recruiting and training young people for political life.

For this third edition, the author has extensively restructured the study to incorporate the experience of the 1980 and 1984 elections and recent additions to the literature on presidential campaigns. The concluding chapter "Why Great Men Are Not

Chosen Presidents," has been adapted from a chapter that appears in another Brookings book, *Elections American Style* (1987). The author expresses his appreciation to the editor of that work, A. James Reichley, and to David S. Broder, Walter Dean Burnham, Milton C. Cummings, Charles O. Jones, Robert A. Katzmann, Herbert Kaufman, Paul E. Peterson, and Donald E. Stokes for their helpful comments.

Thomas E. Mann, director of the Brookings Governmental Studies program, advised on the manuscript. The author is also grateful to James Schneider, who edited the book; to Diane Hodges, Vida Megahed, and Eloise Stinger for administrative assistance; and to interns Jon Buffington and Sarai Brachman.

The opinions expressed in this essay are those of the author and should not be ascribed to the trustees, officers, or other staff members of the Brookings Institution.

BRUCE K. MACLAURY
President

October 1987
Washington, D.C.

Contents

☆ ☆ ☆ ☆ ☆ ☆ ☆ ☆ ☆ ☆ ☆ ☆ ☆ ☆ ☆

ONE Introduction

I LIKE politicians.

Some are bright, some are dim; but as a group they strike me as more alive than most people. Perhaps it is merely the nature of their work. They have to engage us to get elected and hold office. Still, this is a matter of self-selection: no one has to be a politician.

In an essay about how we choose presidents it is useful for the reader to know the direction from which the writer is coming.

Having spent my adult life in Washington, by choice, and having had something to do with four presidents,[1] one of whom was forced to resign the office, I still contend that our country's political class is capable of producing adequate leadership. We do not have to seek out auto company executives or university administrators to ride to our rescue.

This is not an essay on aesthetics. Selecting a president is not a pretty process, and H. L. Mencken found the nominating convention an easy target: "It is vulgar, it is ugly, it is stupid, it is tedious. . . ."[2] But choosing a president does not need to be

1. My assignments have included White House speechwriting (1958–61) and postpresidential services for Dwight Eisenhower; for Richard Nixon, prepresidential speechwriting, deputy assistant to the president for urban affairs (1969), and national chairman, White House Conference on Children and Youth (1970–71); for Gerald Ford, prepresidential speechwriting, presidential appointments to UNESCO and the United Nations General Assembly (1974, 1976), and editor-in-chief of the Republican platform (1976); and for Jimmy Carter, prepresidential adviser on White House transition and consultant on reorganization of the Executive Office of the President (1977).

2. Quoted in Malcolm Moos and Stephen Hess, *Hats in the Ring* (Random House, 1960), p. 15.

1

pretty. I am concerned only with whether it works, not how it looks.

And in considering whether it works, I am skeptical of quick fixes, of proposals that put a patch on party rules or juggle delegate selection timetables or outlaw negative ads. I am a convert to this view, a development that should be obvious to anyone who has read this book's first edition, published in 1974. The nation was then in the wake of Watergate, and the times seemed to demand that we "do something." Some of the things we attempted to do became so mangled in the process of enactment that they created a new set of problems. (Campaign finance laws fit into this category.) Some notions survived intact and turned out to have deleterious consequences. (Midterm party conventions fit into this category.) Austin Ranney is surely right that "the time has come to declare a moratorium on further tinkering. . . ."[3]

Finally, I am an optimistic fatalist. God looks out for the United States. This is unprovable and, given some of our recent history, will be disputed, but, I suggest, it is the healthiest approach to this subject.

The American presidential campaign, at one time or another, has been criticized as encouraging the survival of the unfittest, as wearing out the voters and thus discouraging their attention, as being too focused on political sparring and not enough on issues, and as obscuring any possible perception of candidates' potential mettle. This essay explores these contentions.

It begins with a discussion of what politics can do for us and the way Americans view politicians, especially the irony of a nation that respects its leaders and yet is repulsed by the way leaders become leaders. The examination of political leaders then considers whether professional politicians are the people best able to cope with the stresses and realities of the presidential office.

In chapter 3, "Presidential Qualities," I look at the attributes that are particularly useful in discharging the duties of the

3. "Farewell to Reform—Almost," *Society*, vol. 24 (May–June 1987), p. 29.

presidency and describe the qualities that transcend the temporal and the ideological, that can fit a conservative president as comfortably as a liberal president, and that can apply in periods of social change and conflict as well as in periods that demand consolidation and restoration of order.

The political backgrounds of candidates is the subject of chapter 4, "Routes to the Presidency." Since almost all candidates are professional politicians, does it make any difference whether they have been governor, senator, or vice president? Chapter 5, "Candidate Selection," then focuses on the campaign itself. Does this year-long, sometimes stylized, sometimes impromptu process really inform us whether the candidates have the requisite political, executive, and personal qualities previously defined as presidential?

While the campaign is the means through which the electorate acts as a gigantic search committee, there are other campaign functions (chapter 6) as well. They largely have to do with the development and explication of issues. Is the reasonable discussion of issues, as Theodore White once claimed, merely "the dream of unblooded political scientists"? And what about the campaign as entertainment, which was an important function in the nineteenth century?

"Candidates and Media" (chapter 7) suggests that when we receive information in new ways and that when candidates deliver messages in new ways, new possibilities for distortion may creep into the system. To what extent do media consultants and ad campaigns manipulate the voters and to what extent do journalists affect election outcomes?

Another changing element in presidential elections is the relationship between candidates and parties (chapter 8). Contests between the nominees are also contests between the political parties. What are the consequences of the widening gulf between party organizations and their standard-bearers? Between voters and parties?

The final chapter returns to the various themes of the essay by looking back on the work of Lord Bryce, who a hundred years ago claimed to answer "Why Great Men Are Not Chosen Presidents."

The history of presidential campaigns, as James W. Ceaser has pointed out, is usually divided into five periods based on how the candidates have been selected: the electoral college (1789–92); the congressional caucus (1800–20); the "pure" convention system (1836–1908); the mixed system (1912–68), in which the delegates were chosen by caucus, an instrumentality controlled by party regulars, and by primaries open to rank-and-file voters; and the plebiscitary system (1972–present), with the majority of delegates pledged to candidates through primary elections in which television replaces other means of reaching voters.[4]

What is obvious about this scheme is that during the first two periods, coinciding with the lives of the nation's founding generation, any system would have produced the same presidents. Of dispute is whether since then the different systems have produced different types of presidential candidates. It is the overwhelming judgment of political science and political journalism that they have. It is the theme of this essay that they have not. Indeed, the only major change in candidate type had nothing to do with a selection process. Rather, in the period starting with Andrew Jackson and ending with Theodore Roosevelt, the nation had a fondness for military heroes. Regardless of repeated changes in how we pick presidential candidates, the candidates turn out to be very much alike. *Plus ça change, plus c'est la même chose.*

4. "Improving the Nominating Process," in A. James Reichley, ed., *Elections American Style* (Brookings, 1987), pp. 35–37.

TWO Political Leaders

WHILE abroad on the business of his country during the American Revolution, John Adams wrote to Abigail, "I must study politics and war that my sons may have liberty to study mathematics and philosophy. My sons ought to study mathematics and philosophy . . . in order to give their children a right to study painting, poetry, music, architecture."[1] Thus is politics located on a scale of intellectual disciplines by the man who was to become the second president of the United States. Politics is one of the lower rungs on the ladder of human endeavor; it is not a profession that discerning parents would wish for their children and grandchildren.

The profession of politics, it is true, is not designed to attract the intellectual or the person of genius, although an occasional crisis, usually associated with nation building or nation preserving, may divert a Washington or a Lincoln into political life. Such people must be thought of as exceptional. The founding politician differs markedly from the following politician. The one who comes first, by pioneering a new design or order, can be described as engaging in a creative activity substantially different from the activities that occupy subsequent politicians unless subsequent activities determine whether the nation will survive.

Yet the irony of Adams's ranking of the professions is that politicians generally have greater influence on our daily lives than philosophers and poets. Little wonder, for "political activity

1. Quoted in James Truslow Adams, *The Adams Family* (Little, Brown, 1930), p. 67.

is dangerous. Arising inevitably out of men's ability to influence each other, conferring upon them the benefits of joint endeavor, an indispensable source of social boons, it is also capable of doing great harm."[2] And presidents "can and do hurt people, just as they can and do contribute to social progress."[3] Americans, therefore, must consider seriously the question of their political leadership, especially at the presidential level. Indeed, this becomes increasingly important as the society becomes more statist and vests more power in the executive, and in times of external threat or internal division.

To understand the place of political leadership, it is helpful to sort out what politics is all about. Bernard Crick defines it as "the activity by which differing interests within a given territory are conciliated."[4] Michael Oakeshott judges it "the activity of attending to the general arrangements of a set of people whom change or choice have brought together."[5] Politicians help to lessen the frictions caused by conflicting interests rubbing together. Their job is to devise governmental solutions that are the least unsatisfactory to the most people. When demands are infinite and resources are finite, politicians are at hand to do the allocating.[6]

At most, politicians' claim to creativity arises from their recognition of solutions that are in advance of their constituencies' perceptions and their success in selling their ideas to the electorate. "The creative leader in the long run seeks to broaden the

2. Bertrand de Jouvenel, *The Pure Theory of Politics* (Yale University Press, 1963), p. 29.
3. James David Barber, "Strategies for Understanding Politicians," *American Journal of Political Science*, vol. 18 (May 1974), p. 450.
4. *In Defense of Politics* (Pelican, 1964), p. 167.
5. *Rationalism in Politics* (Basic Books, 1962), p. 112.
6. But what is it that government cannot do? Says Daniel P. Moynihan, the Harvard professor who became a U.S. senator, "It cannot provide values to persons who have none, or who have lost those they had. It cannot provide a meaning to life. It cannot provide inner peace. It can provide outlets for moral energies, but it cannot create those energies." See *Coping* (Random House, 1973), p. 256.

environmental limits within which he operates," according to James MacGregor Burns.[7]

Rarely does the politician create ideas in the way a painter or a poet is creative. The origin and the evolution of ideas or solutions in politics, more often than not, are obscure. This applies equally to the proposals of legislative politicians and of executive politicians. In tracing the development of ideas in the federal executive branch, Adam Yarmolinsky concludes that government serves "as a conduit for ideas from outside." "The greatest source" of ideas is the academic community; they often are "ripened for consideration as government programs" by "a productive interaction between the academic community proper and the worlds of the private research organizations, foundations, and professional associations. . . . Relatively few ideas seem to come from within government itself."[8]

Legislative politicians are instead expected to shape what is present into a form that better fits what is needed, just as executive politicians are expected to grasp the legislative intent and see that it is carried out. Politics, above all, is a group enterprise, which also distinguishes it from most undertakings associated with genius.

Though politics may not be a calling of genius, it is, as John Adams noted, useful and necessary, a profession to be neither revered nor reviled. Indeed, a nation that reveres its political class fails to properly place the order of talents involved; but one that reviles its politicians fails to comprehend the utility of the services they perform.

Americans have always been ambivalent about the political class. In announcing his 1986 list of men most admired by the American people, George Gallup, Jr., said, "Political figures have tended to dominate these lists [since their inception in the mid-1940s]. . . . Sitting presidents of both political parties usually, but not always, have occupied the number one position—as President Reagan has during his tenure. Sen. Edward Kennedy has been among the top 10 for 15 consecutive years." At the

7. *Roosevelt: The Lion and the Fox* (Harvest Books, 1956), p. 486.
8. "Ideas into Programs," *Public Interest*, vol. 1 (Winter 1966), pp. 73–74.

same time, wives of politicians do very well on the list of most admired women. Such polls may merely reflect prominence in the news media, though only one actor and no athletes appear on the lists released in 1987.[9] More likely, they are a mirror of Americans' high opinion of elected public officials. Other polls, however, reflect a low opinion of politicians. "What are we to make of this?" asks Austin Ranney. "Is it good to be an elected official, but bad to do the organizing and campaigning necessary to win office? It seems inconsistent and unfair."[10]

There are forces in society that tend to overemphasize the place of political leaders. Only slowly have educational institutions passed beyond the pedagogic tradition of the great-man-as-history, abandoning their focus on what Sidney Hook calls "the heroic content of historical education."[11] Journalism is geared to report political events, not to identify social and cultural forces. As the managing editor of the *Washington Post* told his staff in 1964, "There is a chilling suspicion that while *The Washington Post* as presently constituted would have reported what Russell and Palmerston said and did in 1848 and 1859 in Commons, it might not have noted a publication by Marx and a book by Darwin in those years."[12] Then, too, the elevation of political leaders undoubtedly serves some psychological needs—security, the quest for authority, compensation for personal limitations, even flight from responsibility—particularly in periods of great stress. No wonder almost every nation has some figure known as the father of his country.

9. "Reagan and Iacocca are 'Most Admired Men,'" *The Gallup Poll*, March 1, 1987; and "Mother Teresa, Margaret Thatcher Are 'Most Admired Women,'" *The Gallup Poll*, February 26, 1987. The list includes Nancy Reagan, Betty Ford, Jacqueline Kennedy Onassis, and Jane Fonda.

10. *Curing the Mischiefs of Faction: Party Reform in America* (University of California Press, 1975), p. 53.

11. *The Hero in History* (Humanities Press, 1943), p. 8.

12. Quoted in Leon V. Sigal, *Reporters and Officials* (Heath, 1973), p. 187. However, using the front page of the *New York Times* (1965, 1975, 1985) as an index, it is clear that there is a growing number, perhaps a third, of nongovernmental stories on such subjects as business/economics, religion, and science/medicine. See Stephen Hess, "Making News in 1985," *Baltimore Sun*, January 5, 1986.

But at the same time, the idiom of the American language clearly reflects a strong bias against politics. The low esteem for the profession is shown in such phrases as "playing politics," "merely politics," and "taking politics out of politics." It has been called a "necessary evil." Compromise, the feature that most characterizes political action, is looked upon as the antithesis of idealism or standing up for principle.

How deeply the cult of antipolitics is ingrained in the United States can be seen in the book that won a Pulitzer prize for one of the nation's most successful politicians. The underlying premise of John F. Kennedy's *Profiles in Courage* is that the courage of their convictions can lead to defeat. One of those profiled, Edmund G. Ross, courageously voted against the impeachment of Andrew Johnson and was not reelected to the Senate. Courage and politics were juxtaposed as incompatible. (Kennedy knew better: the book's first chapter is an eloquent catalog of the politician-legislator's obligations—often competing, often contradictory—to nation, state, constituency, family, and self.)

A distrust of politicians can be detected in the Constitution, for the Founding Fathers designed a form of government in which it is inordinately difficult to lead. When a system of separation of powers, with its checks and balances, is imposed atop the complexities of a democratic state, political executives often find themselves without the authority to match their responsibility. Louis W. Koenig's comment that Washington, Jackson, Lincoln, Wilson, and the Roosevelts interpreted the powers of the presidency "with maximum liberality" is a reminder that presidential greatness often has been achieved by bending the constitutional mandate.[13] And the Twenty-second Amendment, limiting a president to two terms, which was added to the Constitution in 1951, is more recent notice that Americans do not want their politicians to be too powerful for too long.

One way that we partly reconcile our mixed feelings about politics and government is by honoring nonpolitical politicians.

---

13. *The Chief Executive*, rev. ed. (Harcourt, Brace and World, 1968), p. 11.

These are the "citizens" who run for office because they claim to be like us; they leave our ranks for a short time to take their turn at representing us, but they expect to return. The quintessential statement of this attitude was made by Ronald Reagan when he first ran for governor of California in 1966. "I am not a politician," said the future president. "I am an ordinary citizen with a deep-seated belief that much of what troubles us has been brought about by politicians; and it's high time that more ordinary citizens brought the fresh air of commonsense thinking to bear on these problems."[14]

Who best understands us? A question of special interest to voters in a democracy. When it was discovered that Senator Joseph Biden, a candidate for the 1988 Democratic presidential nomination, had plagiarized a paper as a law student, the cochairman of his Iowa campaign reasoned, "I think America is going to relate to Joe Biden because he's an average person. . . . Being an average person means that sometimes you do things below average, and you sometimes do things above average."[15] The senator nevertheless dropped out of the race.

Through much of U.S. history, serving in a legislature was part-time work; sessions were short and legislators derived most of their income from other employment. To some extent this is still true at state and local levels. And in both state and federal governments there are appointed politicians, those who serve in cabinet and subcabinet jobs, who are often amateurs in politics. On the national elective level, however, this is not true. Congress meets year-round and its members are paid accordingly. There is no longer a tradition of short service and rotation in office. The people who become president of the United States have almost always spent a great many years in politics and allied professions. There has not been a truly reluctant presidential nominee (with the possible exception of Adlai Stevenson in 1952)

14. Quoted in Stephen Hess and David S. Broder, *The Republican Establishment* (Harper and Row, 1967), p. 263.

15. Paul Taylor, "Biden Admits Plagiarizing in Law School," *Washington Post*, September 18, 1987.

since the Democrats picked Horatio Seymour, a candidate so
genuinely opposed to making the race in 1868 that he was heard
sobbing to a friend, "Pity me, Harvey, pity me."[16] It is not a
scene easily associated with any recent contenders; contemporary
candidates run long and hard and of their own free wills. The
United States now has a full-time political class and, unless
something strange happens, out of it will come future presidents,
a point I will return to in the final chapter.

To claim that those who seek full-time employment through
elective politics are no different from other citizens is to deny
that there is a self-selective process at work in any occupation.
For doctors, lawyers, accountants, certain aspects of their jobs
attract those of similar aptitudes, skills, and personalities. The
variations may be considerable, and different people may be
attracted by different aspects, but doctors are more likely to be
like other doctors than like engineers. So, too, with politicians.

There are, of course, many reasons why people choose a
career in elective politics. Some are strongly motivated by family
tradition; even in a democracy there is a surprisingly large number
of people for whom politics is the family business. When Albert
Gore, Jr., announced his candidacy for the 1988 Democratic
presidential nomination, the New York Times reported that his
father, who has spent thirty-two years in Congress, "virtually led
the cheering today as he stood proudly behind his son on the
courthouse steps in this town [Carthage, Tennessee] at the heart
of the family's political base."[17] Some conclude that politics is
financially rewarding. Others are attracted to the intellectual
challenge or have deep commitments to ideas, duty, community.
Politicians, in other words, have the same kinds of motivations
as people in other professions—scientists, for example, who "may
be most variously motivated—by a disinterested desire to learn,
by hope of economic gain, by active (or, as Veblen calls it, by

16. Malcolm Moos and Stephen Hess, *Hats in the Ring: The Making of
Presidential Candidates* (Random House, 1960), p. 17.
17. E. J. Dionne, Jr., "Gore, Entering 1988 Race, Projects 'New South'
Image," *New York Times*, June 30, 1987.

idle) curiosity, by aggression or competition, by egotism or altruism."[18]

But since Freud introduced the vocabulary of psychology, political motivation has been described primarily in terms that were invented to explain mental illness. Many political scientists, influenced by the pioneering work of Harold Lasswell, view the politician as a person of low self-esteem. Politics is a vehicle for overcoming early feelings of deprivation. Lasswell's prime type is the agitator, who uses politics to draw attention and affection to himself: "The politician displaces his private motives upon public objects and rationalizes the displacement in terms of public advantage. When this emotional and symbolic adjustment occurs in combination with facility in the acquisition of manipulative skill, the effective politician emerges." Such psychological characteristics need not produce poor leadership. Lasswell cites Lincoln, "plagued by insomnia, feelings of inferiority, of bearing too much responsibility, of pessimism."[19]

Psychologically oriented studies of the political class tend, however, to focus on politicians who have problems. Just as the psychiatrist's couch is not the place to look for people who are "well," psychobiography is rarely about the politician who is "normal." Moreover, the value of psychological studies, more than with most forms of research, depends on the unique insights of the scholar. Like the little girl with the curl, when such studies are good, they are very, very good; they also can be egregious nonsense, perpetrated by writers with flawed knowledge of politics or psychology. Even the best works run the risk of being misread. A superb book on Woodrow Wilson argues that he had an "underlying need for domination," a term that laypersons may associate with pathology.[20] So scholarship of this sort can become

18. Robert K. Merton, *Social Theory and Social Structure*, rev. ed. (Free Press, 1957), p. 532.

19. *The Political Writings of Harold D. Lasswell* (Free Press, 1951), pp. 411, 412.

20. Alexander L. George and Juliette L. George, *Woodrow Wilson and Colonel House* (John Day, 1956), pp. 320–21.

the victim of a popularization process, one by-product of which is the notion that elective politics is the survival of the unfittest.

The psychology of the abnormal might also be drawn on to explain why people run for office. If politics is primarily thought of as a dirty business, no sane person would be expected to spend a lifetime in it. The wife of Earl Long, a Louisiana governor, confirmed that view when her husband was committed to a mental institution: "They say that when Earl gets out of the hospital he will take his certificate of health and take it out on the campaign trail with him. Then he can say he is the only man in the race who can actually prove he is sane."[21]

Political life can strain the ego severely. In most other enterprises there are built-in consolation prizes; the business executive who does not become president of the company can be vice president. But the politician who is not elected is defeated, rejected by peers. Though some very strange people have risen to great heights in politics, generally the politicians who rise on the elective scale have developed unusual abilities to cope with the stresses of political life. They seem to be equipped to reconcile divergent points of view and to deal with ambiguity, long hours, unreasonable demands, and repeated obstacles and challenges. Are these traits associated with low or high self-esteem? The political process tends to screen out people who cannot survive in an ego-bruising world. Hence political leaders are not distinguished as healthier or less healthy than other citizens but as people who have made the best adjustments to the demands of seeking and holding public office.

The politician who aspires to be president has usually climbed the pyramid of elective politics. In the United States there are 7,461 state legislators, 435 members of the U.S. House of Representatives, 100 U.S. senators, 50 governors, 1 president. Not all presidential nominees have mounted each step, but in the modern era all except Eisenhower and Wendell Willkie, the businessman who won the 1940 Republican nomination, can be

21. Blanche Long, "His Wife's Story of the Commitment," *Life* (June 15, 1959), p. 36.

considered professional politicians who served a political apprenticeship of one sort or another. There is evidence that the
winnowing process includes screening out some candidates who
are psychologically least fit.[22]

At the same time, success in politics demands a single-
mindedness with little room left over to cultivate other interests.
This is a highly competitive business, and, as Richard Reeves
said of Franklin Roosevelt, the successful politician is not
necessarily "your basic nice guy."[23] Richard Nixon's pursuit of
the presidency appeared so joyless that some of his friends have
even concluded "he didn't like people." Bryce Harlow told an
interviewer, "I suspect that my gifted friend somewhere in his
youth, maybe when he was very young or in his teens, got badly
hurt by someone he cared for very deeply or trusted totally—a
parent, a relative, a dear friend, a lover, a confidante. Somewhere
I figure somebody hurt him badly, and from that experience and
from then on he could not trust people."[24]

The higher a politician attempts to climb, the greater the
chances of falling. The member of the U.S. House of Representatives who runs for the Senate is a classic case. Most House
seats are safe; most Senate seats are not. Because House members
are elected every two years, representatives who choose to run
for the Senate must relinquish their places. While the reward is
great, the risk is total, as when John F. Kennedy gave up his
assured House seat in 1952 to challenge a popular incumbent
senator, Henry Cabot Lodge. A person who risks so greatly
probably has unusual self-confidence. Given the ethos that

22. For example, James David Barber's study of freshmen representatives in
the Connecticut state legislature concludes that those with the highest self-esteem,
those who work best with others and make the most significant contributions,
appear most likely to continue to pursue a political career and presumably would
be the best bet to get elected to higher office. See The Lawmakers (Yale University
Press, 1965), pp. 224–25.

23. "The Prime-Time President," New York Times Magazine (May 15, 1977),
p. 18.

24. Kenneth W. Thompson, ed., The Nixon Presidency: Twenty-Two Intimate
Perspectives of Richard M. Nixon (University Press of America, 1987), pp. 9–10.

Americans honor in their history and their commerce, it would be surprising if they did not also reward risk-takers in politics.

Moving from state legislature to national legislature to White House (or some variant, which may include a governorship or the vice presidency) will not impress every observer as a Darwinian progression. Many share H. L. Mencken's view of the politician as "a sturdy rogue whose principal, and often sole aim in life is to butter his parsnips."[25] Yet it is certainly a long, usually tortuous climb, during which successively larger constituencies have the opportunity to judge the politicians' fitness, greater attention is paid them by news media and opponents, wider scope and greater detail are added to their records of performance, and their skills are honed by practice. The least fit might survive the process; the chances, however, are far greater that they will not. Like any system, this one is best judged by the odds it offers.

Still, if presidents prove inadequate to the circumstances of history that confront them, we should look for clues in the qualities required of them and the extended path candidates must travel to get to the White House. But regardless of the rules of the road, they travel within a context that stretches over 200 years of Americans' ambivalence toward politics and politicians—from John Adams' wish for his sons to rise above politics to Ronald Reagan's belief that our troubles have been brought about by politicians—coexisting with a professional political class on whom the nation must rely for leadership.

25. *Notes on Democracy* (Knopf, 1926), p. 99.

THREE Presidential Qualities

☆ ☆ ☆ ☆ ☆ ☆ ☆ ☆ ☆ ☆ ☆ ☆ ☆ ☆ ☆ ☆

MAX FRANKEL, executive editor of the *New York Times*, told his staff in 1987 that American presidents "have no 'right' of privacy. Their lives, their personalities, their finances, their families, friends and values are all fair game for fair reporting."[1] Indeed, in this discussion of what qualities a president should be expected to have, being a public person heads the list. That means more than being capable of holding public office and assuming public responsibilities. Presidents must be willing to be exposed, to become a public property, different only in degree from the White House in which they sleep and work and may have to raise their children. The people have the right of inspection, and those places that are put off limits are automatically suspect. The exposure of the president may be akin to a perpetual house and garden tour, with a steady stream of strangers passing through, fingering the furniture as well as the presidential ego. As television reporter Sam Donaldson told President Carter, "We're going to cover you one way or the other."[2]

The loss of privacy is nearly total. Presidents' pasts are a matter of open discussion. When they are ill, their bodily functions are the subject of news briefings. Their friends become celebrities by definition, their families monuments on which the public can scrawl graffiti, even their dogs the First Dog. This extension of the presidency to include the president's private life is a twentieth-century phenomenon; there is nothing comparable in the earlier

1. Eleanor Randolph, "Questions Too Pointed, N.Y. Times Editor Says," *Washington Post*, June 20, 1987.
2. Sam Donaldson, *Hold On, Mr. President!* (Random House, 1987), p. 16.

history of the country. It is a by-product of breakthroughs in communications technology: as the means and capacity to distribute information increased, making the information business highly profitable, presidents, their families, and their friends became the raw material that fuels a major industry. The trend is irreversible.

The loss of privacy necessarily becomes intimately bound up with the conduct of the office. Any description of the political techniques employed by presidents would differ little from those of corporate executives, union leaders, or academic administrators. All these leaders, in essentially the same manner, offer rewards or withhold rewards, with varying degrees of subtlety; all, in essentially the same manner, assess the strengths and weaknesses of supporters and opponents; all seek ways to build constituencies and to minimize opposition. What differs is the public aspect of presidential politics. The politics of business, union, and university are essentially private—played out within the confines of boardroom, union hall, and faculty commons. The U.S. Senate provides a public platform for its members, but Senate politics, conducted in cloakroom and conference committee, also are relatively private. Only presidents must have the ability to conduct their business without a hiding place. Thus the presidential quality of being a public person, which assumes a willingness to abandon the sense of privacy, becomes essential to the operation of democratic government. No open society can afford a private presidency. The openness of the presidential office is the best insurance that there will be no dark corners where Watergate-type corruption can breed and that public policy will be properly ventilated before being approved.[3]

Presidents must have high intelligence: receptivity to new ideas, ability to absorb complex thoughts, capacity to distill ideas to their essence. This raises the question of what specific knowledge they should have to perform their duties. Theodore E. Sorensen, who was President Kennedy's top White House aide, stated that

3. But see Anthony Lewis, who writes, "The loss of respect for privacy has exacted a terrible price in American politics." *New York Times*, May 5, 1987.

the president "must be at home with a staggering range of information. . . . He must know all about the ratio of cotton acreage to prices, of inventory accumulations to employment, of corporate investment to earnings, of selected steel prices to the economy, and of the biological effects of fall-out to the effects of natural radiation."[4] This image of the presidency as requiring an intellectual Hercules is unfair to the person in the White House and to the electorate. It is untrue that presidents need know "all about" an almost infinite range of recondite matters, any more than university chancellors need know all about macroeconomics, clinical psychology, microbiology, and linguistics to run their institutions. What presidents need know is whose advice to seek: can one person give full and dispassionate information, or should competing experts be consulted? Which subjects are important now, and which may be important in the near future? When must decisions be made? What might be the consequences if no decision is made or if someone else is allowed to make a decision? These, rather than the ratio of cotton acreage to prices, are the sorts of things presidents need know.

Yet Sorensen is correct if he means that a president's intelligence must be broadly based. Above all, presidents should have wide interests and concerns. The problems of the country are diverse and interrelated. Presidents must indeed respond to particular crises as they arise and often must compartmentalize their attention to conform with governmental timetables—there is a time to prepare a budget, a time to deliver the economic report to the Congress, and so forth. Nevertheless, it is only the ability to keep many balls in the air that can harmonize national needs and aspirations. Richard Nixon, a man of high intelligence and narrow interests, became almost totally consumed with matters of foreign policy during his first term. In delegating responsibility for matters not directly related to foreign policy he abandoned the oversight of activities in which corruption then developed. Bill Moyers, who was President Johnson's press

4. *Decision-Making in the White House* (Columbia University Press, 1963), pp. 38–39.

secretary, suggests that something similar occurred in the Johnson White House during the winter of 1965, when the crucial decisions were made to escalate the war in Vietnam: "The President was—we were all—caught up in presenting the Great Society legislation to Congress. . . . Vietnam seemed to be more of a nuisance than a menace."[5] A scholar finds that President Kennedy, "viewing Berlin as his big problem, perhaps did not have a great deal of residual energy to invest in staffing out Vietnam."[6]

The electorate has a right to expect certain executive talents in all presidents. Many scholars, however, have downgraded these skills. James MacGregor Burns goes so far as to completely separate leadership from management. Leaders, he thinks, should be concerned with "goals rather than methods"; executive qualities are "secondary matters."[7] None of the seven qualities singled out by Clinton Rossiter in his famous book on the American presidency is executive.[8] But presidents reside at the top of a vast enterprise. Their primary executive skills will be in choosing personnel and arriving at decisions. Some people can make up their minds about complex matters faster than others. Some have instincts—and the luck—that enable them to pick the right people for the right jobs, to find advisers who compensate for their own weaknesses, to get people to work together for a common cause, and to know when to discipline their subordinates.

Presidents must choose the decisions they wish to make. They cannot possibly make all decisions in an undertaking that employs more than 5 million people. They must not be "nibbled to death by the guppies of minor or marginal issues," as presidential adviser Bryce Harlow once put it.[9] Nor can presidents allow

5. "Bill Moyers Talks about LBJ," *Atlantic* (July 1968), p. 30.
6. Richard Tanner Johnson, *Managing the White House* (Harper and Row, 1974), p. 148.
7. See *Presidential Government* (Houghton Mifflin, 1966), pp. 194–95.
8. See *The American Presidency* (Harcourt, Brace and World, 1960), pp. 172–74.
9. Quoted in Emmet John Hughes, *The Living Presidency* (Coward, McCann and Geoghegan, 1973), p. 342.

themselves to be overtaken by events and swept along by the actions of subordinates. They should populate the White House with advisers capable of sorting out problems for their attention; they should appoint department and agency heads who can manage their operations effectively and represent the president faithfully to the Congress, the bureaucracy, and their constituents. Presidents must resist the temptation of allowing the White House to become "operational"—as the Tower Commission explained after the fact to Reagan in 1987.[10] At the same time, they must resist being captured by the departments' perceptions of reality. They must arrive at decisions and make them known in ways that do not undermine those who must carry them out. Presidents must also prod appointees and civil servants to provide better information, more efficient operations, and more humane services. All of this must be done without the tools most executives in the private sector have. Government responds more to persuasion than to hierarchal command, its funding is not under executive control, and its employees are largely outside the president's power to hire and fire.

Depending on the problems that urgently call for attention in their administrations, presidents may benefit from the expertise they bring to the office. Dwight Eisenhower's military background was uniquely suited to making cuts in the defense budget after the Korean War. Especially in conducting foreign policy—given the speed of events, the potential gravity of acting or not acting, and the secrecy often required—chief executives will be particularly advantaged by specialized knowledge. Nixon's extensive travels in Asia led to reopening relations with the People's Republic of China. Lyndon Johnson, however, had little experience with or interest in foreign affairs when he came to office. In his

10. President Reagan appointed a special review board (known as the Tower Commission) to study White House involvement in the "Iran/contra matter." On February 26, 1987, it recommended that the National Security Council staff should no longer "engage in the implementation of policy or the conduct of operations. This compromises their oversight role and usurps the responsibilities of the departments and agencies" (p. V–5 of the report to the president).

handling of the Vietnam War, the problem was not that the president received one type of advice exclusively. The Defense Department pressed for increased involvement and the Central Intelligence Agency reported that the war was not going well. Perhaps U.S. commitments in Vietnam might have been of a different order if Johnson had had a background more suited to weighing the competing advice he was given.

High intelligence should not be confused with intellectuality, which need not be a presidential quality. Indeed, an intellectual may be at some disadvantage in the White House. Wilson, the former professor who envisioned a League of Nations as the foundation of world peace, refused to make the concessions necessary to get his treaty through the U.S. Senate. The intellectual may have difficulty translating thoughts into the common idiom; or may be removed by class and background and experience from the immediate concerns that presidents are expected to deal with; or may be incapable of taking prompt action because of a disinclination to base decisions on imperfect information or reduce complexities to terms that can be dealt with in the political process. It was Harry Truman, a nonintellectual, who won the praise of European statesman Jean Monnet for having "the ability to decide."[11] The best definition of the democratic statesman remains Bagehot's "an uncommon man of common opinions."[12]

Presidents must have a transcending honesty. After a period of corruption, integrity may be sufficient reason to elect a person, and the act of being honest may be deemed an important public service, as it was in the presidencies of Calvin Coolidge and Gerald Ford, which followed major scandals, Teapot Dome and Watergate. But the electorate does not confuse honesty with ability. The same principle applies to courage. Presidents must

11. See John W. Gardner, *Attributes and Context: Leadership Papers*, 6 (Washington, D.C.: Independent Sector, 1987), p. 6. Note, for example, Truman's decision to use the atomic bomb: "Let there be no mistake about it. I regarded the bomb as a military weapon and never had any doubt that it should be used." Harry S. Truman, *Memoirs*, vol. 1: *Year of Decisions* (Doubleday, 1955), p. 419.

12. Harold J. Laski, *The American Presidency* (Harper, 1940), p. 37.

have the courage to swim against the tide, the courage to take unpopular actions, and the courage not to act, which sometimes can be the greatest courage of all. John Adams had the courage not to go to war with France, for example, after the XYZ Affair, which appeared to be a French demand for a bribe from the U.S. government. But presidents can also make courageously bad decisions. Some have put Kennedy's Bay of Pigs decision in this category.

What presidents need even more than honesty or courage, however, is the type of sensitivity that "Uncle Joe" Cannon, a Speaker of the U.S. House of Representatives, felt comes from having ears full of grasshoppers because they are so close to the ground. They must have a feel of the nation—understand the people's hopes and fears—and have a strong sense of the concrete. They must understand that they preside over a nation of individuals and that their policies affect people individually.

Yet almost everything that happens after a new president steps inside the White House makes it difficult to consider individual reactions. Information is collectivized: the goods that workers produce and the services they perform become the gross national product; people become the raw data for tabulations, percentages, and trends. What presidents know of the American people they must learn before they reach the presidency. Once surrounded by the Secret Service and the Signal Corps and reporters, they will continue to be seen by the people, and occasionally even be touched by the people, but they will learn about them primarily through the media, the public opinion polls, and their advisers inside and outside of government. They will stop learning directly from the people.[13]

Political intuition tells presidents whether they must inch toward a goal or will be able to strike boldly, how flexible to be,

13. Patricia Schroeder worries that this separation now extends to the presidential selection process as well. When declining to seek the Democratic nomination she said: "I could not figure out how to run and not be separated from those I serve. . . . I could not bear to turn every human contact into a photo opportunity." See T. R. Reid, "Schroeder Rules Out '88 Bid," *Washington Post*, September 29, 1987.

and how best to deploy their powers to gain the support they need. There is a sharp edge to the political qualities that we expect in our presidents. We expect them to maneuver, compromise, arm-twist, threaten—all in our best interests. These are standards of behavior that differ markedly from those we value in our personal relations. They are difficult to bring into harmony with ethical teachings. Of all twentieth century presidents, the two Roosevelts came closest to having the kinds of political qualities that allowed them to perform their duties most effectively.[14] Both were seekers of power with a single-minded intensity, experts at manipulation, with the ability to reverse field quickly. We might have desired them to be people of inestimable goodness as was William Howard Taft. But it was advantageous to the nation that the Roosevelts were master politicians, whereas Taft's personal goodness proved only modestly useful in the absence of political skills.

The Roosevelts also were strongly exhibitionistic. Not all presidents have to have their well-developed dramatic instincts and their appreciation of the mysteries of making news. But all presidents must find ways to communicate, to persuade the people, and to arouse and enlist support. Ronald Reagan has been derisively called "The Great Communicator" by his detractors, but the appellation reflects the fact that he possesses a unique presidential quality.

The ability to use the White House to create consensus, ease fears, and restore confidence—that is, to communicate—assumes a style that is acceptable to a majority of the people. Past presidential styles have varied from the laconic leadership of Coolidge, to the calm grandfatherliness of Eisenhower, to the boyish exuberance of Kennedy. But at a minimum, presidential style assumes a background without serious blemishes or, since there is a sort of statute of limitations in politics, only blemishes of ancient vintage that have been expiated or excused by the electorate. Every year some library committee takes offense at books by a James Joyce or a Henry Miller, but despite the Mrs.

14. Erwin C. Hargrove, *Presidential Leadership* (Macmillan, 1966). p. 146.

Grundy image of America as a nation of official puritans, Americans have consistently shown a sophisticated view of sexual conduct as a potential disqualification for the presidency. Comments and speculation on intimate relationships have sometimes figured in presidential campaigns: Jefferson and a black slave; Jackson's wife, who was a bigamist; Cleveland's illegitimate child. Still, never has that aspect been a determining factor. Even Gary Hart's decision to leave the Democratic presidential race in 1987 had more to do with his exercising bad judgment than with his offending the electorate's sense of acceptable sexual behavior.[15]

Shady financial dealings have been far more decisive, as best illustrated in the contest of 1884, when Grover Cleveland, who was accused of fathering a bastard, ran against James G. Blaine, who was accused of receiving a veiled bribe from an Arkansas railroad. In that election, a Chicago man wrote to a newspaper, "I gather that Mr. Cleveland has shown high character and great capacity in public office but that in private life his conduct has been open to question, while on the other hand, Mr. Blaine in public life has been weak and dishonest while he seems to have been an admirable husband and father. The conclusion that I draw from these facts is that we should elect Mr. Cleveland to the public office which he is so admirably qualified to fill and remand Mr. Blaine to private life which he is so eminently fitted to adorn."[16] The voters agreed.

Presidents can wear loud sport shirts or lose their tempers at music critics, as Truman did when his daughter Margaret's singing received a bad review. Such actions might even increase their popular standing unless they are seen as compromising effective presidential behavior. Decorum is not automatically equated with solemnity or middle-class behavior. While we are basically a middle-class country, we have elected and taken pride

15. See "Gary Hart's Judgment," *New York Times*, May 5, 1987; also Mark J. Penn and Douglas E. Schoen, "The Issue Is Not Morality: It's Candor," *New York Times*, May 6, 1987.

16. Quoted in Sidney Hyman, "Scandal Following Script," *Washington Post*, October 18, 1964.

in a collection of patrician presidents. Presidents need not be like us, and it may help if they are not, if only because we think it less likely that the rich will steal from the public till. A show of wealth does not offend most of us, perhaps because most of us would like to be wealthy, or because we may think that wealth imparts special talents to those who have made it or good omens to those who have been born with it—especially since by seeking elective office the rich are asking to serve us, asking to be commoners. When Pierre S. du Pont IV, a former governor of Delaware, announced that he was seeking the 1988 Republican presidential nomination, the *New York Times* reported that he "bears one of the most illustrious names in American business" and that he "prefers to be known as Pete."[17]

A more subtle presidential quality is a sense of history. Not a reliance on history "to make the most of precedents established by his predecessors, and to see in the problems confronting him replicas of problems confronting chief executives in the past,"[18] for precedents are always available to buttress a position, and history repeats itself only in the most general terms. Rather, a sense of history that provides the understanding of what must be preserved and protected in the country, such as individual freedom, human dignity, and political democracy. It is an understanding of history that locates for presidents where they fit into the constitutional scheme of things, keeping them in phase with the other forces in government so that they operate as neither steamroller nor pushover in their relations with the Congress, courts, and states. In this sense, a president's understanding of history becomes a restraint on despotism.

This historical sense should also provide the perspective to resist fads and passions of the moment. Unfortunately, the "exalting thought that he sits in Lincoln's seat"[19] is capable of

17. E. J. Dionne, Jr., "Du Pont Enters the G.O.P. Race for President," *New York Times*, September 17, 1986.

18. Joseph E. Kallenbach, *The American Chief Executive* (Harper and Row, 1966), pp. 265–66.

19. Rossiter, *The American Presidency*, p. 136.

producing a touch of megalomania in a president. American history, with its play of fortuity, should be more humbling.

The ultimate usefulness of a president's personal qualities is to inspire public trust. This is not the same as being loved or noncontroversial. Nor can it be defined solely by style or personality, although style and personality can help inspire trust; nor by programs or ideologies, although these too help. It does not mean trust by everyone but by enough citizens to ensure that the social fabric will remain intact and that some effective action can be taken. Some equate trust with lack of pomp and recommend establishing it by abolishing "the 21-gun salutes, the honor guards, the red carpets, the elaborate state dinners, the Presidential hideaways."[20] This was the logic behind many of the symbolic acts taken by President Carter early in his administration, such as his limiting the number of White House limousines and the playing of "Hail to the Chief." However, Herbert Hoover's loss of trust was hardly due to excessive pomp, and the disposing of presidential yachts by Kennedy and Nixon did not measurably affect the people's trust in them one way or another.

The elements that go into inspiring trust are a style that is not offensive to the majority, a transcending honesty, a high level of intelligence, a willingness to deal with problems that immediately touch people's lives, a sense of patriotism, and a public confidence in those to whom presidents lend their prestige and authority.[21]

20. John Reed, "Pomp and Politicians," *New York Times*, December 8, 1972.

21. Some presidential campaigns—Andrew Jackson's in 1832, John Kennedy's in 1960, Ronald Reagan's in 1984—have been based largely on a sense of patriotism. Kennedy said in the final televised debate, "I don't believe that there is anything this country cannot do. I don't believe there's any burden or any responsibility that any American would not assume to protect his country." *Freedom of Communications*, Part III: *The Joint Appearances of Senator John F. Kennedy and Vice President Richard M. Nixon and Other 1960 Campaign Presentations*, S. Rept. 994 (GPO, 1961), p. 276. Jesse Jackson announced his candidacy with these words: "There is something wrong with our government policies today. . . . But there is nothing wrong with America. America is our land. America is God's country. America has been blessed and God bless America." See Paul Taylor, "Jackson Opens '88 Bid Atop Democratic Polls," *Washington Post*, October 11, 1987.

What we expect in presidents we also expect in those around them, though to a lesser degree. This encompasses their families and associates in descending order of importance down to members of their political parties.

Finally, to aspire to more than adequacy, presidents must dream grandly, have goals and direction, and, if possible, offer concrete proposals when they take office. Yet this is not necessary for every president; there are moments that call for marking time, for consolidation. One problem with many theories of the presidency is the assumption that all presidents must be heroic and must interpret their powers with "maximum liberality."[22] But all presidents should desire to leave the nation better than they find it, should be able to push to some degree against the limits of what is considered feasible, and should have a generosity of spirit that seeks to bring out what is best in the people.[23]

22. See Louis W. Koenig, *The Chief Executive*, rev. ed. (Harcourt, Brace and World, 1968), pp. 11–12; Arthur M. Schlesinger, Jr., *The Crisis of Confidence* (Houghton Mifflin, 1969), p. 298; and James MacGregor Burns, *Uncommon Sense* (Harper and Row, 1972), p. 172. This view of the "strong, heroic" president largely was based on scholars' infatuation with Franklin Roosevelt and was particularly in vogue during the 1950s and early 1960s. The Vietnam War caused a reassessment of the presidential office. See George E. Reedy, *The Twilight of the Presidency* (World, 1970); Henry Fairlie, *The Kennedy Promise* (Doubleday, 1973); Eugene J. McCarthy, *The Year of the People* (Doubleday, 1969), esp. pp. 294–95; and Barbara W. Tuchman, "Should We Abolish the Presidency?" *New York Times*, February 13, 1973.

23. For a comprehensive list of thirty-two "attributes of presidential leadership" prepared by a veteran journalist who was also an adviser to President Carter, see Hedley Donovan, *Roosevelt to Reagan* (Harper and Row, 1985), pp. 295–309. One presidential quality that perhaps we can take for granted is stamina. Presidents are elected to lead the government and we expect them to have the energy to match the task. A new counterwisdom, however, contends that no president ever died of overwork. George E. Reedy, for instance, graphically shows that the president's days are as painless as staff, technology, and creature comforts allow. See his *The Twilight of the Presidency*, pp. 4, 21. Historically the point is well taken: James K. Polk came closest to working himself to death, and even he survived his presidential term. Indeed, Thomas A. Bailey computed that when assassinations are factored out, presidents have lived beyond their actuarial life expectancy. See his *Presidential Greatness* (Appleton-Century, 1966), pp. 340–43.

FOUR

Routes to the Presidency

☆ ☆ ☆ ☆ ☆ ☆ ☆ ☆ ☆ ☆ ☆ ☆ ☆ ☆ ☆ ☆ ☆

RATHER than develop criteria of qualities a president must have, those who picked presidential candidates before the proliferation of state primary elections in the 1970s followed certain rules of availability, that is, political qualifications for winning, not presidential qualifications for governing. In 1954 the British scholar D. W. Brogan summarized the common characteristics that the so-called kingmakers looked for in major party nominees:

> The candidate must come from a state with a large electoral vote and from a state that is not certain to vote for the party candidate. . . . These considerations have ensured that, in this century, only one candidate has been nominated from a small state, Mr. [Alfred M.] Landon of Kansas in 1936. . . .
>
> No congressional leader of the very first rank, save James Madison, has ever been elected President. . . . For in Congress, it is often necessary to take a line; to choose sides. The leading congressional candidates are almost certain to have angered some group, injured some interests, to be associated with some legislation or with opposition to some legislation that may, so the timid fear, cost many, many votes in a presidential election. . . .
>
> After the defeat of Governor [Alfred E.] Smith in 1928 it is unlikely that a Catholic will be nominated in the foreseeable future and a fortiori a Jew or a Negro is ruled out on the simple grounds that such a nomination would alienate more voters than it could possibly gain. . . .
>
> There are, of course, more specific forms of availability than being a male Gentile, White, Protestant from a large and doubtful state. In this century, there is no doubt what office provides the best springboard for a presidential candidate. It is being or having been

(being is much better) Governor of a large, doubtful state, especially the State of New York.[1]

Since 1954, the common assets that Brogan identified have been notably altered. No longer is it necessary to come from a large state. Recent major-party nominees have been residents of Arizona (Barry Goldwater, 1964), South Dakota (George McGovern, 1972), Georgia (Jimmy Carter, 1976, 1980), and Minnesota (Hubert Humphrey, 1968; Walter Mondale, 1984). Moreover, candidates seeking 1988 nominations are from Arizona (Bruce Babbitt), Delaware (Pierre du Pont), Kansas (Robert Dole), Missouri (Richard Gephardt), and Tennessee (Albert Gore, Jr.), and it can be said with certainty that none will be rejected on the basis of place of residence. Neither party in recent years has been greatly influenced in its nominations by the doubtful state, for each party now has carried the electoral vote of every state at some time (although the Republicans have not carried the solidly Democratic District of Columbia). Moreover, of course, network television is not bounded by state lines.

All major-party nominees between 1960 and 1972 had served in the Senate, and since 1960 only Carter and Ronald Reagan had never been elected to Congress. A Catholic was elected president in 1960,[2] a black ran a serious campaign for the Democratic nomination in 1984, and a woman was her party's vice presidential nominee that year.

In his summation Brogan might have noted that presidential candidates were usually in their fifties or early sixties and that rarely was a losing nominee given a second chance (Grover Cleveland, William Jennings Bryan, and Thomas E. Dewey were the only modern exceptions to the latter rule at the time his book was published). Since 1954, however, three nominees have been in their forties, one has been in his seventies, and two previously

1. D. W. Brogan, *Politics in America* (Harper, 1954), pp. 197–200. The paragraphing has been added.

2. It has been argued that the Democrats would have had their best chance of winning in 1972 if they had nominated a Catholic. See Louis H. Bean, *How to Predict the 1972 Election* (Quadrangle, 1972), pp. 84–85, 218.

defeated candidates have been given renominations. In an electoral sense, what John F. Kennedy did in 1960 for Catholics and youthful contenders, Ronald Reagan in 1984 did for senior citizens, and Richard M. Nixon in 1968 did for losers.

The best place from which to wage a campaign for president has not been a state house but the White House—at least until 1976, when Gerald Ford barely survived a nomination challenge from Reagan and then became the first incumbent to lose the presidency in forty-four years. Four years later Reagan defeated President Carter. Increasingly incumbency must be looked upon as double-edged: presidents take credit for everything that goes well during their years in office, whether they deserve credit or not, and they will be blamed for what goes wrong, whether they are at fault or not.[3]

The 1976 contest was further distinguished because two contenders—Carter and Reagan—were politically unemployed when they sought presidential nominations. While senators and incumbent governors were tied down by legislative sessions and other duties, the two former governors were making a full-time job of running for president, as did former Vice President Walter Mondale in 1984. Seeking the nomination has become an enterprise that involves putting together a sizable organization, campaigning in more than thirty state primaries and in the caucus states, preparing media presentations, and raising millions of dollars. Some politicians, such as James R. Thompson of Illinois, even contend that it is impossible to be a sitting governor and a successful presidential nominee.[4] Howard Baker, Gary Hart, and Paul Laxalt declined to seek reelection to the Senate on the grounds that if they were to become contenders for the 1988 nomination it would consume all their energies. Yet when Donald Rumsfeld, a former secretary of defense, aborted his campaign in 1987, he claimed that only the holder of a powerful

3. See Stephen Hess and Thomas E. Cronin, "The Incumbent as Candidate," *Washington Post*, August 20, 1972.
4. See David S. Broder, "Our Peculiar Way of Picking Presidents," *Washington Post*, March 1, 1987.

public office, such as a congressional committee chairman, has the necessary clout to raise enough money to make a successful race for president.[5] And additionally, after Hart dropped out of the contest, his campaign manager concluded that being a U.S. senator is worth "$2 million for a presidential campaign. One million in salaries and one million in equipment, WATS lines, word processors and desks. Everyone in the office is working on the campaign to a greater or lesser extent."[6]

In recent years the system of presidential selection has been under great pressure to change. It has proved highly adaptable and it has, indeed, changed. But nominees continue to come mainly from the Senate, the vice presidency, and governorships. All other sources—the cabinet, the House of Representatives, mayoralties, and nongovernmental jobs—appear to be poor routes to the nomination. When senators dominated the selection process in the 1960s, the reasons given were the flow of power to Washington, with its vastly expanded federal budget and proliferation of grant-in-aid programs; the serious political liabilities governors accrue in trying to perform their duties, in contrast to the dissipated blame that legislators share for governmental failures; the ability of those in the nation's capital to dominate the news, in part because Washington is the news center of a truly national communications medium; a lessening of party control over the nominating process; and the predominance in American life of international issues that are outside the purview of state leaders. When governors reasserted dominance with the nominations of Carter and Reagan, the reasons given were

5. See Karen Diegmueller, "Underfunded Dreams Die Fast in Race for the Oval Office," *Insight* (May 4, 1987), p. 18. Moreover, wrote Richard L. Berke in the *New York Times*, September 1, 1987, "The Democrat whose fund-raising has most impressed his rivals is Mr. Dukakis, who has already collected an estimated $5 million. His success has been largely attributed to his position as the only incumbent governor in the race. Of the $4.6 million his campaign raised as of June 30, about 70 percent came from Massachusetts residents, including top real estate executives who do business with the state."

6. See Howard Kurtz, "Campaign Blurs Roles of Biden Aides," *Washington Post*, June 21, 1987.

Washington's failures, notably the Vietnam War and the Watergate scandal, and an ideological shift away from centralizing governmental power.[7]

Those senators who successfully aspire to presidential nominations are neither the ordinary legislators, who stick close to constituent problems and keep low profiles, nor the giants of the Senate. The record of legislative leaders who have caught White House fever is one of total disaster—Champ Clark, Oscar Underwood, John Nance Garner, Alben Barkley, Robert Kerr, Arthur Vandenberg, Robert Taft, William Knowland, Lyndon Johnson (1960), Wilbur Mills, Morris Udall, and Henry Jackson. Republicans Howard Baker and Robert Dole fell by the wayside in 1980, as did Democrats Ernest Hollings and Alan Cranston in 1984. Moreover, when Lyndon Johnson became president by accident in 1963, the skills and habits that he brought with him from his Senate years were not an unalloyed blessing. Johnson did get his "Great Society" program through the Congress in 1964–65, in sharp contrast to his predecessor, John Kennedy (who had not been a leader in the Senate), but the traits of the cloakroom often worked against Johnson and made him suspect in the eyes of the public and the press. A president cannot afford to appear too devious in manner or ingenious in device. There is a difference between legislative intrigue and presidential intrigue; Franklin Roosevelt was a genius at the latter and failed notably when he attempted the former. Leadership in the closed society of the Senate, with its accepted traditions of bargaining, "creative compromise," and petty favors, when transferred to the presidency can create a dangerous attitude of "every man has his price." Usually the legislators who get presidential nominations are those who have not subscribed to the folkways of the Senate: long

7. See Robert L. Peabody, Norman J. Ornstein, and David W. Rohde, "The United States Senate as a Presidential Incubator," *Political Science Quarterly*, vol. 91 (Summer 1976); and Richard E. Cohen, "As a Launching Pad for the Presidency, Congress Isn't What It Used to Be," *National Journal*, March 8, 1980.

apprenticeships, dull legislative spadework, unhurried delibera-
tion, heavy specialization.[8] Rather, they are what their colleagues
scornfully call "show horses" or "grandstanders."

The vice presidency emerged as an important source of
nominees largely because of Dwight Eisenhower's distaste for
partisan politicking and the fortuitous coupling of the second
oldest president in history with the second youngest vice president.
Franklin Roosevelt had begun the practice of giving special
assignments to vice presidents, and Harry Truman's sudden
assumption of the presidency had increased awareness of the
importance of preparing the vice president. But no president
before Eisenhower gave his vice president as many chores or as
much exposure. Turning the vice president into an instant
celebrity and a chief party spokesman guaranteed that Richard
Nixon would have a head start on the next available presidential
nomination. The prominence of the vice presidency then increased during the incumbencies of Hubert Humphrey, Walter
Mondale, and George Bush.[9]

Yet seldom are vice presidential candidates chosen because of

8. See Donald R. Matthews, *U.S. Senators and Their World* (University of
North Carolina Press, 1960), esp. chap. 5. Senator Robert Byrd, Democrat of
West Virginia, lists the traits necessary to be a good Senate leader as "patience,
good temper, fairness, knowledge of the members and ability to organize them,"
which, as I have outlined, are different from the traits needed in presidents. See
Jacqueline Calmes, "Byrd Struggles to Lead Deeply Divided Senate," *Congressional Quarterly* (July 4, 1987), p. 1423.

9. The vice presidency can also be an extremely difficult position from which
to win elections. Writing of Vice President Humphrey's race for the presidency
in 1968, Edmund Muskie said that he "had none of the advantages that an
incumbent President usually enjoys. . . . He was seeking ways to make himself
an independent candidate, to be his own man, without being disloyal [to
Johnson]." *Journeys* (Doubleday, 1972), p. 54. The dilemma is apparent in
Nelson W. Polsby's partisan effort to define Humphrey's views: "It would not be
correct to say that [Humphrey] has been important in the making of Vietnam
policy." *The Citizen's Choice: Humphrey or Nixon* (Washington, D.C.: Public
Affairs Press, 1968), p. 35. Similarly, in 1987, referring to the Iran-contra affair,
Vice President Bush said, "When you don't know something, it's hard to
react. . . . We were not in the loop." See David S. Broder, "Bush Asserts
Vindication in Iran Affair," *Washington Post*, August 6, 1987.

their qualifications for assuming the presidency. Their selection is a prerogative of the presidential nominee, who usually aims at balancing the ticket. The balance may be ideological (Wendell Willkie–Charles McNary, 1940), geographical (Kennedy-Johnson, 1960), religious (four of the last six Democratic pairings have been Catholic-Protestant or vice versa), or efforts to heal party wounds by choosing the runner-up (Bush, 1980). The most obvious balance, of course, is gender (Geraldine Ferraro, 1984). The vice presidential nomination may be part of a deal to assure the presidential nomination (Franklin Roosevelt–John Nance Garner, 1932) or may even be calculated to detract least from the ticket (Nixon–Spiro Agnew, 1968).[10]

The backgrounds of vice presidential nominees are somewhat different from those of presidential nominees. Candidates for the vice presidency are more apt to have held high appointive office (Secretary of Agriculture Henry Wallace and Peace Corps Director Sargent Shriver); to have been party officers (Republican National Chairmen William Miller, Robert Dole, and Bush); to be younger, less experienced legislators and governors (Nixon, Eagleton, Agnew, Ferraro); and even, on rare occasion, to have come from outside the political ranks (Frank Knox, a newspaper publisher).

The assassination of John Kennedy, the resignation of Richard Nixon, the mental health record of Thomas Eagleton, and the corruption of Spiro Agnew should be a warning that a vice presidential selection deserves serious attention. Walter Mondale was chosen with great care in 1976, but only because Jimmy Carter's nomination had been assured well in advance and there was ample time to sift the qualifications of potential running mates. Eight years later, when Mondale was the presidential nominee, he did not do as careful a check into Geraldine Ferraro's

10. A *New York Times* editorial (August 24, 1972) contended that Nixon in 1968, knowing he would run less well with a prominent partner than by himself, "chose Mr. Agnew because he was the closest he could come to a political cipher." On balancing "Washington insiders and outsiders," see Paul C. Light, "Making the Most of the New Vice Presidency," *Brookings Review* (Summer 1984), p. 20.

background, and the news media subsequently raised questions about her family's ties to organized crime figures.[11]

When Eagleton's nomination for the vice presidency was withdrawn in 1972, the Democrats stumbled into a different and superior way of choosing a candidate. The national convention authorized the party's national committee to convene a few weeks after the close of the convention for the purpose of selecting a vice presidential candidate. Such a delay gives presidential nominees an opportunity to consider their recommendations carefully. It also allows time to test the sentiment of party professionals, sample public opinion, and investigate the backgrounds of potential candidates. Moreover, potential candidates can wage a short campaign by appearing on nationwide television programs and by other means of public exposure. A delayed vice presidential selection permits the final session of the national convention to focus solely on the attributes of the presidential nominee, and by giving another responsibility to the national committee, it may have the effect of strengthening the party system.

Other means have been proposed for reforming vice presidential selection. One would have the presidential nomination precede approval of the platform, thereby giving the nominee an extra day to weigh vice presidential alternatives. Another would add a day to the normal convention calendar. A plan put forward by Ronald Reagan in 1976 would have required presidential candidates to announce their choices for vice president before the convention begins. It was voted down by the Republican convention and is unlikely ever to be accepted, largely because it narrows the options of the party's standard-bearer. A useful variation, not unduly restraining on the candidates, might require presidential contenders, after the last primary, to release lists from which their vice presidential nominee would be drawn.[12]

11. See Albert R. Hunt, "The Campaign and the Issues," in Austin Ranney, ed., *The American Elections of 1984* (Duke University Press, 1985), p. 155.

12. See James I. Loeb, "On Nominating a Vice President," *Washington Post*, January 27, 1974; Warren Weaver, Jr., "Change Proposed for Picking

No change should be made in the system that would replace the presidential nominee as the key decisionmaker in selecting the running mate. Any method that encourages the nomination of a vice president who is out of phase with the chief executive should be viewed with skepticism. The task is to find ways to help the presidential nominee give the proper time and thought to this crucial choice.

Some commentators feel, however, that the present system should be retained exactly because it forces the presidential nominee to decide under pressure. If a potential president is "incapable of making a prudent judgment on his running mate" under existing time constraints, "I would have very strong reservations as to how he would handle himself in a conference with Mr. Brezhnev or if there were a series of crises around the world," said former presidential press secretary George Reedy in 1977. "I think we get a little too obsessed with orderly procedure sometimes, and assume virtues to orderly methods of doing things that may not necessarily be there."[13]

Is there any background that is most likely to produce a skillful president? The Senate, although it has been called a vocational school for presidents, confers no special presidential skills on its members except possibly the habit of taking a national point of view. (What the Senate does give aspirants is a grand platform from which to launch a campaign for the White House.) The vice presidency, with its collection of minor bureaucratic duties, offers no special training in presidential skills, although it provides a useful opportunity to observe a president in action from close range. A governorship affords executive experience, which neither the Senate nor the vice presidency does, but usually fails to provide international experience.

G.O.P. Running Mate," *New York Times*, January 18, 1980; and Stephen Hess, "How We Might Have Avoided Spiro Agnew," *Baltimore Sun*, February 15, 1980.

13. Quoted in Alan L. Otten, "Spare Tire," *Wall Street Journal*, April 14, 1977.

It might be helpful for a president to have been both senator and governor. (Between 1977 and 1987, twenty-three U.S. senators had previously served as governors of their states. Also, there are presently six governors who have been members of Congress.) However, some doubly qualified candidates are too old to meet effectively the demands of the presidency. A U.S. senator or governor with cabinet experience, say, as secretary of state, might be successful. But this would have made James Buchanan the ideal candidate for president. The least qualified elected president would have been Abraham Lincoln (who served one term in the House of Representatives and was defeated in his race for the Senate). Theodore Roosevelt chose Lincoln and Buchanan to illustrate the right and wrong ways to be president. [14]

It is not surprising that television has figured prominently in the fates of modern candidates—Estes Kefauver's televised Senate committee hearings on organized crime in 1950, Nixon's "Checkers speech" in 1960, various campaign debates, Edmund Muskie's speech on the eve of the 1970 congressional elections that propelled him into the front-runner slot for the 1972 Democratic presidential nomination. But Lincoln's fortunes were equally affected by a debate, Charles Evans Hughes's by an investigation of corruption in New York life insurance companies, and William Jennings Bryan's by his "Cross of Gold" speech. Candidates evidently employ—successfully or not—the tools of communications at hand. And the types of people who run for president in the television era are not recognizably different from those who ran in earlier times. Nor has television altered the nature of the issues in presidential campaigns. While TV does seem to favor the interests of senators whose faces are more often seen on the network news and the Sunday interview programs, governors quickly catch up once the presidential primaries begin, and place of domicile ceases to be a consideration.

Over the years the kinds of experience potential presidents

14. See Wayne Andrews, ed., *The Autobiography of Theodore Roosevelt* (Octagon Books, 1975), p. 198.

have had have changed from time to time—sometimes favoring senators and vice presidents, sometimes favoring governors. While governors and senators are not entirely interchangeable, they probably are among that subset who also have presidential ambition. The system continues to produce the same types of people: whether senators, governors, or vice presidents, those who become nominees of the major parties are professional politicians. What they all have in common is that they have run for office successfully. The qualities that make them successful politicians are different from those that bring success in other professions. Thus the nonpolitician generally is excluded from the presidential selection system. Here, as in all professional selection systems, an apprenticeship, a pretesting, is demanded of those who attempt to reach the top of the profession. The only other widely used occupational avenue to the presidency has been the military, also a public profession, which produced a lot of presidents in the nineteenth century, but only Dwight Eisenhower in the twentieth.

The system, however, is not entirely closed. The one exceptional outsider was Wendell L. Willkie, a utilities company executive, who became the Republican party's nominee in 1940. As early as 1937 a columnist in the Worcester, Massachusetts, *Telegram* suggested that Willkie would make a good candidate. Eventually other columnists, such as Arthur Krock of the *New York Times* and Raymond Moley in *Newsweek*, began referring to him as a presidential possibility. Willkie made impressive guest appearances on popular radio shows ("Town Hall" and "Information Please"); his writings turned up in major magazines (*Fortune, Reader's Digest, Atlantic Monthly*); and he addressed such influential groups as the American Newspaper Publishers Association.[15] But even then Willkie's nomination was possible only because of a conflict between Thomas Dewey and Robert Taft over which he had no control. Yet in terms of his own

15. See Herbert S. Parmet and Marie B. Hecht, *Never Again: A President Runs for a Third Term* (Macmillan, 1968), pp. 62, 70, 84, 88, 90, 91.

behavior, Willkie was acting as a politician, and his success attested to his professionalism.

The traditional ladder to the presidency is to start early in elective politics. It has been a rule of thumb that a nonmilitary person does not get to be president unless he has run for something before the age of thirty.[16] There is also a two-step process, however, in which an astronaut like John Glenn or an actor like Ronald Reagan first achieves recognition outside the political arena and then turns to elective politics.

Hardly a presidential campaign goes by without some newspaper editorial bemoaning the system's failure to recruit the "best and the brightest"—some citizens' advocate or distinguished intellectual or superstar of the business world. The name most often mentioned for 1988 was Lee Iacocca.[17] Yet the attractiveness of such figures is often based on their not having had governmental responsibilities. If suddenly thrust into the White House, they would not lose their intelligence, but they would lose their political virginity. Like every past president, they would have to adjust to the needs of the broadest audience and the restraints of the narrowest audiences. This does not imply that business executives, union leaders, academics, and so forth should not seek the presidency, but that nonpoliticians should be tested through an essentially political process. It is likely that professional politicians are best prepared for the presidency, a political office, because they are the most skillful at reconciling the divergent needs of the many groups and interests that look to government for support. Our presidential selection system offers a wide choice among professional politicians. At the beginning of each election cycle there are generally about eight candidates in the out-party, fewer in the in-party where there may be a first-term incumbent

16. Carter's abbreviated career in the navy somewhat delayed his entrance into politics, but otherwise his progress—state legislator, governor, president—conforms with the rules of political progression.

17. See "The Implications of Iacoccamania," *American Political Report*, vol. 16 (September 19, 1986), pp. 1–4.

or an obvious heir apparent. Some political scientists even believe that there are too many contenders for the voters to make rational choices.[18] But if the menu of choices does not include the best and the brightest, the failure lies in how society attracts its citizens into the political profession.

18. Donald R. Matthews has noted, "Our present nominating procedures were severely strained . . . by the unusually large number of rather evenly matched candidates the Democrats had in 1972. It is hard to imagine the chaos that might have ensued if there had been two or three times more." My own view is that the candidates in 1972 and since then have fallen by the wayside quite naturally (sometimes even gracefully). A plethora of candidates, as Matthews envisions, however, could strain the capacity of the news media on which we rely for our political information. See Matthews's essay, "Presidential Nominations: Process and Outcomes," in James David Barber, ed., *Choosing the President* (Prentice-Hall, 1974), p. 41.

FIVE Candidate Selection

☆ ☆ ☆ ☆ ☆ ☆ ☆ ☆ ☆ ☆ ☆ ☆ ☆ ☆ ☆ ☆ ☆ ☆

OSTENSIBLY conducted to inform voters, to allow them to see all sides of an issue, in effect to elicit the truth, campaigns instead seem to do the opposite: they can make truth more obscure. But is there a better way, and, if so, what is the appropriate amount of time that the nation should devote to choosing its president?

Part of the problem is that presidential campaigns operate under a law of contradictions. Campaigns, from the viewpoint of the candidates, are expected to produce an approximation of truth through the clash of contending forces. But candidates are under no obligation to state the weaknesses of their own positions or the strengths of their opponents'. Truth may be on both sides of an argument, on neither side, or partly on each side.

An adversary process works better in jurisprudence, probably because of differences between the courtroom and the campaign. In the courtroom the issues are limited and carefully prescribed; the number of participants is few; the traditions of behavior and standards of admissibility are established and enforceable; the verdict is usually negotiable; the advocates—lawyers, not defendants—are relatively disinterested parties; and the decision is based on a determination of fact or law. None of these conditions exists in the adversary proceedings of politics: the issues are whatever each side and outside observers choose, and rarely are they the same for each side or each voter; the players are many and confusing, and though there may be only two major presidential candidates, they address the electorate through many representatives. Moreover, there are concurrent elections at many levels with all sorts of overlap in issues, organizations, and personnel. The tradition of civility is weak; indeed, tradition often works the other way—candidates have always attributed malevolence to their opponents. There is no enforcer or judge other than the ultimate election-day judgment of the voters, and this comes too late to ensure a high standard of campaign conduct. There is no possibility of compromise or negotiation, for a candidate must either win or lose. And the determinants are not merely facts (even if the facts could be agreed upon), but also personality, emotion, instinct, and other intangibles, all of which have a legitimate place in elections.

So the adversary system is not well designed to inspire trust in future presidents or encourage them to dream grandly, qualities that we have identified as presidential. With the candidates snapping at each other's heels, there is little incentive to develop broadly based programs that differ markedly from the status quo. It is a system that is at its best at exposing the candidates' deficiencies, both personal and programmatic.

It is possible to design an election system in which a greater variety of truths is presented, in which there is a greater likelihood that each voter could find a political stance more closely approaching his or her view of the truth. A multiparty system would offer such diversity, but it would make governing the country infinitely harder. For when each truth becomes a political party, truths harden into moral absolutes. And what honorable person is willing to split the difference between right and wrong?

However, under the present system parties mainly wish to attract enough voters to gain the magic 270 electoral votes. The quintessential political nature of this process allows the country to expect that presidents will be finely attuned to the decibels of public opinion, that they will operate within the perimeters of acceptability and at a pace best geared to winning support for their proposals, and that they will know how to use the tools of public persuasion and legislative maneuver.

Having succeeded in climbing a political ladder, however, is no guarantee that a president will seek the sorts of political solutions that promote the greatest progress and the least rancor. Because of flukes of circumstances or for other reasons, at least three twentieth century presidents have not been instinctive politicians. William Howard Taft, at heart, was a judge, Herbert Hoover a technocrat, Richard Nixon a secretary of state. Dwight Eisenhower has often and incorrectly been put in this category because he had never sought elective office and had an aversion to partisan politics. But he was intuitively a brilliant bureaucratic politician whose military experience in World War II had not been as a battlefield warrior but as a political organizer of warriors. Richard Nixon, on the other hand, has often mistakenly been grouped among the political presidents. Indeed, he ran for more elective offices than any other twentieth century president. But he hated the rituals of politics.[1] Though he mastered them, he always felt that they trivialized him. The rituals of the campaign serve a purpose, however; they force the candidate upon the people and the people upon the candidate. Nixon in the White House devoted himself largely to foreign policy. Watergate can be partly viewed as the end result of a process of presidential disengagement from domestic politics. The system ceases to function properly when the checks and balances of politics are removed. Politicians do not burglarize the opposition (if only because the risks of getting caught are too great); politicians do not tap wires (if only because too many people would know and someone would talk); politicians do not let their parties atrophy (if only because they will need party leaders in their debt); politicians do not seek solitude as a way of life (if only because it is through wide contacts that they get votes).

Nixon is a remarkable exception in a system geared to producing political presidents. As a rule the system screens out those who find the selection process distasteful. In an office that must rely on the delicate political antennae of its occupant for effective action, there is reason to be concerned over efforts to further

1. For a different analysis, however, see John Ehrlichman in Kenneth W. Thompson, ed., *The Nixon Presidency: Twenty-Two Intimate Perspectives of Richard M. Nixon* (University Press of America, 1987), p. 137.

depoliticize the system and thereby risk catapulting a person without political instinct into the White House. One proposal to depoliticize the presidency, for example, would limit a president to a single six-year term, thereby eliminating behavior that presumably might be motivated by an incumbent's desire to get reelected: "It is just intolerable that a President of the United States—any President, whatever his party—is compelled to devote his time, energy, and talents to what can be termed only as purely political tasks," said former Senator Mike Mansfield at a Judiciary Committee hearing.[2] But a successful president has to be a successful politician, and politics, though not held in high repute, is an essential part of democracy. A president who is removed from politics will become a president remote from the processes of government and removed from the thoughts and aspirations of the people.

No leadership selection process in any other democratic country is as intensely personal as the American political campaign. The parties provide no protection for their presidential candidates, who must live by their wits. The press is persistent in its demands. The people expect a degree of knowledge about the candidates' private lives that would be considered impertinent in other societies. They may even discover whether a candidate has lust in his heart. By election day the voters have had the opportunity to learn a great deal about the candidates' backgrounds and styles. The question of how well campaigns test for acceptable presidential styles then becomes tautological: presidents must have styles that are acceptable to a majority of Americans; if they can get elected, their styles are acceptable to a majority of Americans.

No political office (not even the vice presidency) can prepare a president for the public exposure of the office. In 1968 Edmund S. Muskie, a senator and a former governor, found that being the Democratic vice presidential nominee was "an exhilarating

2. *Single Six-Year Term for President*, Hearings before the Subcommittee on Constitutional Amendments of the Senate Committee on the Judiciary, 92 Cong. 1 sess. (GPO, 1971), p. 32.

experience."[3] But four years later, when seeking the presidency, he discovered that attacks on his wife were more nightmare than exhilaration.[4] The only testing—and training—for this aspect of the presidency is to run for president. The day a candidate acquires a personal press corps and a Secret Service detail is the day the acclimatization begins.

If just one word could be used to describe the nine-month contest from the Iowa caucuses and the New Hampshire primary in February, through "Super Tuesday" in March and the summer national conventions, to election day on the first Tuesday after the first Monday in November, the word would have to be "ordeal." It requires candidates to raise funds, build staff, delegate responsibilities, allocate resources effectively, plan strategy, select positions, and make instant decisions. They must time and coordinate events, function well under pressure, and take criticism and keep coming back, all without losing touch with people along the way.

It is easy to fail the test. In May 1987 Gary Hart, the front-runner for the Democractic nomination, was reported to have spent a weekend with a woman who was not his wife. He withdrew from the race. In 1972 Edmund Muskie, the front-runner for the Democratic nomination, broke down in "uncontrollable tears that were captured by TV cameras" in replying to a New Hampshire newspaper attack on his wife. He withdrew from contesting primaries.[5] In 1967 George Romney, the front-runner for the Republican nomination, told a television interviewer that he had experienced "the greatest brainwashing that anybody can

3. Edmund S. Muskie, *Journeys* (Doubleday, 1972), p. 57.

4. See David S. Broder, *Behind the Front Page* (Simon and Schuster, 1987), pp. 23–26.

5. Myra MacPherson, "Jane Muskie: A Wife Becomes 'an Issue,'" *Washington Post*, March 12, 1972. Lou Cannon of the *Washington Post* has a fascinating account in *Reporting: An Inside View* (Sacramento: California Journal Press, 1977), pp. 156–57, of covering Muskie in New Hampshire in which he comments on examples of the senator's "temper" that went unreported, presumably because they were outside the press's definition of news. It may thus have been that Muskie's tears—a news event—were used by reporters to symbolize what they felt their readers should know about a potential president.

get when you go over to Vietnam." His ratings dropped sharply in the polls and he withdrew from the race.[6] To say that Hart's adultery, Muskie's tears, or Romney's brainwashing were the reasons for their failures would be misleading; rather, these events became the symbols of their weaknesses in the public mind, weaknesses that became apparent only as a result of the ordeal that is the presidential campaign. Still, in 1976 when Jimmy Carter made questionable remarks about "ethnic purity," he was able to contain the damage and win the nomination and election. In 1984 Ronald Reagan was able to neutralize the issue of possible senility by turning his age into a joke during a TV debate with challenger Walter Mondale.[7] The brutal manner in which some are eliminated and some survive is one of the realities that presidential candidates must accept.

The voters, on their part, face the task of choosing a president on the basis of a record that bears little relation to the crucial decisions that will have to be made in the next four years about matters that are currently unknown. And since circumstances change and crises arise, the dilemma becomes how to judge without certified knowledge. What would a potential president do if North Korea invaded South Korea, or if the East Germans built a wall between East and West Berlin, or if the Soviet Union put offensive missiles in Cuba, or if unemployment and inflation rose at the same time, or if Iranian militants captured the U.S. embassy in Tehran? Massachusetts Governor Michael Dukakis, when declaring his presidential candidacy in 1987, rightly said, "The next President of the United States will face challenges that no campaign position paper can possibly anticipate. But what can be measured in advance is the character of the person who will confront those challenges."[8]

Our system insists that potential presidents run an obstacle

6. See Theodore H. White, *The Making of the President 1968* (Pocket Books, 1970), pp. 71–73; and Louis H. Bean, *How to Predict the 1972 Election* (Quadrangle, 1972), p. 148.

7. See Albert R. Hunt, "The Campaign and the Issues," in Austin Ranney, ed., *The American Elections of 1984* (Duke University Press, 1985), p. 158.

8. E. J. Dionne, Jr., "Dukakis Says He Will Run for President," *New York Times*, March 17, 1987.

course. A candidate, in 1952, suddenly discovers that his running mate has a "secret" fund of $18,000 contributed by wealthy supporters; a candidate, in 1972, suddenly discovers that his running mate has a record of serious mental illness. The candidates must make a decision, quickly, in full public view. Will they retain or replace the vice presidential nominee? And in watching the candidates in the act of making decisions we are given the opportunity to learn something about them, something that is useful in trying to assess how they might respond to sudden crisis if they were in the White House.

There have been more and more complaints that the presidential selection process takes too long. It may be, however, only that recent election campaigns have seemed too long. Consider the interparty phase of the last six elections: 1964 (Johnson-Goldwater), 1972 (Nixon-McGovern), and 1984 (Reagan-Mondale) were landslide victories in which the outcomes were never in doubt; 1968 (Nixon-Humphrey) was a contest between two durable candidates who had been on the national scene for a generation; 1976 (Ford-Carter) was a contest between drab orators. Only in 1980, when Reagan defeated Carter, was there enough drama to keep voters tuned in. Campaigns also may seem longer because television more quickly sates whatever public appetite there is for political fare, while at the same time public opinion surveys have made elections more predictable.

Presidential campaigns, in fact, are not getting longer, although contenders now formally announce their candidacies earlier in order to have more time to raise money.[9] It probably has always been true that the serious candidates began to run in earnest immediately after the preceding midterm election. Andrew Jackson was put forward by the Tennessee legislature three years before the 1828 election. On July 5, 1927, H. L. Mencken wrote in the *Baltimore Evening Sun*, "The chief danger confronting the Al Smith boom lies in the fact that it started too soon"

9. Since the 1976 campaign a partial public financing system has allowed contributions to candidates of $250 or less to qualify for federal matching grants; individuals are allowed to give a maximum of $1,000 to a candidate.

(Smith, of course, won the 1928 Democratic nomination). Campaign manager James Farley spent two years before the 1932 convention rounding up delegates for Franklin Roosevelt. And John Kennedy's drive for the 1960 nomination began in 1956 and has been called "the campaign before the campaign."

After he retired from the White House, Eisenhower argued that campaigns consist of "fairly fruitless words" and could be shortened to thirty days "without changing the result decisively."[10] He was right in that only in very close elections, such as that of 1960, will enough voters make up or change their minds during the "official" campaign (Labor Day through election day) to actually affect the results. For example, pollsters contend that voters in 1972 knew they were going to reelect Nixon even before the Democrats nominated a candidate.[11] But a presidential selection system should not be based on the assumption that every election is going to be a landslide. (In fact, half of the presidential elections in this century have been close calls.)

The reasons most often given for shortening presidential campaigns are that the technology now exists to inform the electorate quickly and that a long campaign bores the electorate, thereby lowering voter turnout. Yet the lowest voter turnout of the modern era (51 percent in 1948) came in an exciting and unpredictable four-way race for president, and apathy has been widely discounted as an explanation for why turnout rates have stayed under 60 percent in recent elections.[12] There is, in fact,

10. See Dwight D. Eisenhower, *The White House Years: Waging Peace, 1956–61* (Doubleday, 1965), p. 18.

11. See Daniel Yankelovich, "Why Nixon Won," *New York Review of Books* (November 30, 1972); and speech by Louis Harris, National Press Club, Washington, D.C., November 10, 1972.

12. See Walter Dean Burnham, "The Turnout Problem," in A. James Reichley, ed., *Elections American Style* (Brookings, 1987). Curtis B. Gans, director of the Committee for the Study of the American Electorate, argues that "election day registration" and certain other changes, such as door-to-door registration, could increase turnout by 10 million voters. See his "Non-Voting," a paper prepared for the Brookings Conference on Party and Electoral Renewal, April 6–7, 1987. However, Alan Ehrenhalt, political editor of *Congressional Quarterly*, says, "I don't assume that greater participation creates better public

little evidence that a low turnout is a product of boredom and a long campaign. Moreover, though television provides the means of informing voters quickly, all voters do not tune in to politics at the same time. Those who are least informed politically are also the least educated and poorest.[13] An election system in a democratic society must allow its least informed members the opportunity to catch up. It is not they but the best informed who most appear to have lost patience with the long process that results in the election of a president. At the same time, the steady disintegration of identification with a political party, which once accounted for 60 percent of voter preference in presidential elections, means that more people now rely on events during the campaign to help them decide. This was certainly the case in 1976 when Gerald Ford came from 30 points behind in the polls to almost catch his rival on election day.

Viewed from the perspective of the candidates, the long campaign also serves as an equalizer. When an incumbent is running, which has been true in two-thirds of the elections in this century, rarely will the opposing candidate be as well known. First-term presidents are running for reelection every day they are in office; their challengers need a campaign to make headline news on a regular basis. They need added time to transmit their ideas and personalities to the electorate, as well as time to build an organization. In effect, the long campaign benefits the underdog.

A short campaign has the added disadvantage for the public that it is easier to manipulate than a long one—candidates have to put greater emphasis on televised campaigning; fewer people have the opportunity to see the candidates in person; it is more difficult to separate the candidates from the creations of their

---

policy. I think it's important for people to have an opportunity to vote. I don't think it's important that they actually do vote in enormous numbers. Communist countries have a turnout of about 95% or higher. That doesn't mean that people are getting the representation that they want." See "An Interview with Alan Ehrenhalt," *Political Report* (May 29, 1987), p. 6.

13. See Angus Campbell and others, *Elections and the Political Order* (Wiley, 1966), p. 136.

ghostwriters and public relations specialists. It is exactly because the campaign is long and arduous that it eventually penetrates into the field of vision of many Americans; the longer the candidates participate in the ordeal, the greater the likelihood that their characters and instincts will be perceived by the electorate.

Shortening the campaign, even if desirable, is far easier to propose than to accomplish. Moving the primaries closer to the conventions or moving the conventions closer to election day—the suggestions most often put forth—would shorten the home-stretch but not the track. Those seeking the presidency would still begin their active quests when it best served their interests. (And recent experience is that candidates improve their chances by getting started earlier.) The only effective way to shorten the campaign would be to abolish the fixed-term presidency, allowing the head of government to call a new election at any time within a given period, as the British do. Such a system would entail additional expense, assuming that other contests were not brought into conformity, would create problems of overheating the political system by increasing the number of elections, and would give a decided advantage to incumbents, who would choose election dates that maximized their chances.

The result desired by opponents of the long campaign might be achieved by limiting the number or timing of candidates' activities, rather than by shortening the number of days. This is a variant of whether a tree falling in the forest makes a noise if no one is around to hear it fall. Does a campaign exist if the candidates are prevented from advertising themselves? One proposal calls for a five-week limit on campaign advertising.[14] But rules of this sort could be challenged in the courts as violations of free speech. The best chance of skirting the constitutional question might be to tie formal limits into optional public financing: candidates who accepted public financing of their campaigns would have to agree to certain conditions, including limits on when the money could be spent.

14. See Bill Brock, "The Money Problem," *New York Times*, May 14, 1973.

Ideally, of course, the campaign should be neither too short nor too long. If we could start again from scratch, an efficient schedule would be to hold state primaries and caucuses in January, February, and March (as we now do), but then move the national conventions to April, with the election in late May or early June when the weather is most agreeable in most of the country and hence the voter turnout might be greater, and then inaugurate the president a month later, perhaps on every fourth July 4. Such a scheme would compress the period from the Iowa caucuses and the New Hampshire primary to the inauguration into less than six months, half the time of the present system.

Americans do not need a presidential campaign to judge the qualities of an incumbent. Voters know what a president has done, and what the president's party has done. The election then serves as a blunt yet efficient instrument for them to decide whether they want to throw the rascals out. According to Aaron Wildavsky, "This instinctive and convulsive changing of the guard need not be caused by a popular belief that the candidate or leaders of one party are better than another. All that is necessary is widespread dissatisfaction and a consequent desire to give a new team a chance."[15] Nor can a fresh candidate avoid the record of an incumbent administration: Adlai Stevenson in 1952 could not dissociate himself from the Truman administration, although he did not serve in it, and Republican candidates will not be able to disengage themselves from the Reagan administration in 1988 even if they choose to. Though there are many ways in which politicians can be held accountable, from impeachment through legislative votes, elections provide the most regularized system of accountability.

Yet a blunt instrument is not necessarily a just tool. Presidents and their parties are blamed (or try to take credit) for everything that happens during their tenure, whether they are responsible or not. Still, there is a certain raw logic for periodically giving a new team a chance regardless of ideology or even a record of

15. *The Presidency* (Little, Brown, 1969), p. 366.

past successes. "I always thought my mind would develop in a high position," said former Secretary of State Henry Kissinger. "But, fatigue becomes a factor. The mind is always working so hard that you learn little. Instead, you tend to work with what you learned in previous years."[16] There are other reasons an administration loses effectiveness as it ages. Lyndon Johnson, a master of congressional relations, knew that he could expect problems with Capitol Hill if he sought and won a second term. "Congress and I are like an old man and woman who've lived together for a hundred years," he told Harry McPherson. "We know each other's faults and what little good there is in us. We're tired of each other."[17] In 1937 Leo C. Rosten could forecast that Franklin Roosevelt, a master of press relations, would encounter difficulties in time: "The [press] corps had greeted Mr. Roosevelt with frenzy in 1933; in it there was a will-to-believe which, because it ignored future possibilities and past experience, would end by tearing down the myth it was creating."[18] Presidents get tired; it becomes harder for them to attract top-level executives to government service; personal and ideological conflicts develop within their administrations; interest groups learn to oppose the president more effectively; the mystique wears off; people get bored. And power starts to drift away if a president cannot or will not run for reelection.

The process for selecting presidents cannot ensure that all will perform their duties well. But the process should at least test those qualities—personal, political, and executive—without which a president could not properly function. The campaign tests a candidate's executive qualities only to the degree that the candidate manages the operation of this fairly modest enterprise, comparable in expenditures and personnel to a relatively small corporation. It hardly touches on those executive qualities, of far greater importance, that are necessary to administer the federal estab-

16. Quoted in Norman Mailer, *St. George and the Godfather* (New American Library, 1972), p. 120.

17. *A Political Education* (Atlantic–Little, Brown, 1972), p. 428.

18. "President Roosevelt and the Washington Correspondents," *Public Opinion Quarterly*, vol. 1 (January 1937), p. 49.

lishment, including the setting and policing of public policy. Questions of management—the structure of governance—are seldom campaign issues; for campaigns are about politics, not governance. Occasionally the argument will be heard that candidates who know how to run a campaign must know how to run the country or, conversely, that candidates who cannot run their own campaign well will not be able to run the country. Every now and then a campaign will be so mismanaged as to make this an issue of sorts. But despite references in the press to the technical proficiency of campaign management, few voters make the connection.

Moreover, executive ability is not primarily what people seek in a president. Mencken wrote of Herbert Hoover's "reputation as a competent and intelligent administrator—which is precisely the last thing that the endless hordes and herds of the common people ever give a thought to."[19] But Mencken misread the intuitive wisdom of the hordes and herds in correctly ordering priorities. Our presidents, more often than not, have been atrocious administrators. They often come from an occupation (legislator) and a profession (law) that ill-prepare them for management. And the similarities between management in the public and private sectors are too tenuous to expect business executives to do much better than legislators. The dilemma of presidents as executives is more likely to be resolved by refining the job description of the presidency than by changing the selection process.[20] After all, the management structure that contributed to producing Watergate was devised by one of the most management-conscious presidents in American history. Perhaps, as George Reedy suggests, "the institutionalized approach tends to drive out the political approach."[21]

19. A *Carnival of Buncombe* (Johns Hopkins Press, 1956), p. 11 (reprinted from *Baltimore Evening Sun*, May 12, 1920). In a similar vein, Alistair Cooke dismissed Thomas E. Dewey as "a fine administrator" in *Listener* (September 10, 1959), p. 376.

20. An attempt to do this can be found in Stephen Hess, *Organizing the Presidency* (Brookings, 1976), esp. pp. 151–52.

21. See R. Gordon Hoxie, ed., *The White House: Organization and Operations* (New York: Center for the Study of the Presidency, 1971), p. 167.

The political qualities of presidential candidates, primarily the ability to gauge public opinion and the skill to win approval for programs, are well tested in the campaign, as should be expected in a system in which electoral success depends on welding so many diverse groups and interests. It is hard to imagine presidents getting elected without having mastered the intricacies of politics. (The problem is that, once elected, they may ignore them.)

The system obviously tests physical stamina, but observers differ on whether it does as well at testing other personal qualities— the ability to perform as a public person, honesty and courage, a style that is acceptable to most Americans, the ability to inspire public trust, and a sense of history that affirms a loyalty to democratic values.

Alternative systems, however, probably would be equally flawed. If the system cannot with equal fairness test the personal, political, and executive talents that are necessary in the White House, the process should give priority to testing the personal. For personal talents are the most immutable, the least likely to be changed by experience in office. Presidents can become politicians and executives; they are not likely to become better persons.

SIX Other Campaign Functions

THE CAMPAIGN is primarily a process of personnel selection, of course. But it is more than the electorate operating as a gigantic search committee. A presidential election also serves as a forum to explicate policy positions, as the excuse for national self-examination, and as entertainment.

Before he dropped out of the race for the 1988 Democratic presidential nomination, former Senator Gary Hart of Colorado declared, "I intend to run a campaign of ideas. . . . Ideas are what governing is all about and governing is what this election is all about."[1] Dealing with ideas and issues is the most faulted part of the campaign process. Yet is "the reasonable discussion of issues," as the late Theodore H. White contended, merely "the dream of unblooded political scientists"?[2]

Some observers have charged that politicians ignore most issues and break their pledges on those they cannot ignore, that the candidates' speeches are exercises in oversimplification, overdramatization, and (if aimed at incumbents) overcatastrophization. The 1932 Democratic platform pledged a balanced budget, and the 1968 Republican platform opposed recognition of Communist China. Franklin Roosevelt unbalanced the budget, and Richard Nixon set up an office in Peking. More recently, David S. Broder

1. Quoted in Alex Brummer, "Gary Hart is Back," *Manchester Guardian Weekly*, April 19, 1987. In almost the same words, Edmund Muskie wrote when he sought a presidential nomination that a candidate "must actually develop proposals, policies, and programs. . . . That is part of what a campaign is all about." *Journeys* (Doubleday, 1972), pp. 50–51.
2. *The Making of the President 1960* (Pocket Books, 1961), p. 351.

reminds us, "Jimmy Carter campaigned for a simplification and decentralization of government and added two cabinet departments. Ronald Reagan campaigned for fiscal austerity and ran up record deficits."[3]

The assumption is that such conduct is wrong, that campaigns should be instruments of precision and intellectual rigor, and that candidates should keep their word. After all, our system must ultimately depend on our faith in words. But overlooked in the critiques is that candidates prefer to keep their word, other things being equal. Roosevelt's pledge to balance the budget does not have to be seen as an attempt to mislead the voters.[4] He may have thought of it as a long-range goal, which he tried to honor by appointing some fiscal conservatives to key posts, such as Budget Director Lewis Douglas, by cutting federal spending when he thought the time was right, as in 1936–37, and by continuing to pledge a balanced budget in the 1936 platform. Or in weighing competing demands, he may have concluded that reducing unemployment deserved a higher priority than balancing the budget. And it is possible that his thinking changed as he was influenced by different economists.

Usually some identifiable event determines why presidents do not honor a pledge: they try and fail (Nixon's resort to wage-price controls to slow inflation); circumstances change (Eisenhower's abandonment of his promise to contain communism when the Hungarian uprising threatened to require U.S. military intervention); or they learn something they did not know (Kennedy's secretary of defense told him that there was no "missile gap," as he had claimed before his election). Rarely do politicians gain, at least in the short run, from changing their minds. Even the candidate whose promises are not made in good faith is alert to the inherent problems of acting against them. Thus as a rule of survival, politicians would rather keep their commitments.

Surprisingly, perhaps, the same can be said of a party's platform.

3. *Behind the Front Page* (Simon and Schuster, 1987), p. 259.
4. See James MacGregor Burns, *Roosevelt: The Lion and the Fox* (Harvest Books, 1956), pp. 167, 171–72, 333.

The platform is an instrument with a bad reputation, "generally regarded as a document that says little, binds no one, and is forgotten by politicians as quickly as possible."[5] But the record is not nearly so dismal. "Only a tenth of the promises are completely ignored," writes Gerald Pomper.[6] After a detailed analysis of recent platforms, candidates' position papers, and speeches, Jeff Fishel concludes, "Every president, from Kennedy through Reagan, has demonstrated considerable good faith, seeking through legislation or executive order to follow through on a majority of his campaign pledges."[7]

Besides trying to tell the voters what the party will do for them, the platform drafters are engaged in a collective bargaining process over the composition of the party. The resultant document allows each group to decide whether it can remain in the coalition. In recent years Democratic platforms have been to the left and Republican platforms to the right of their elected officials. For example, the 1980 Republican platform, for the first time in forty years, did not endorse the Equal Rights Amendment, while the Democratic platform went beyond endorsement, pledging to "withhold financial support and technical campaign assistance for candidates who do not support ERA."[8] The presidential candidate will sometimes have to balance platform promises (a statement of the already committed) with campaign rhetoric (an appeal to the uncommitted).

Occasionally there are major-party candidates whose main purpose in running for president is to educate the voters. Perhaps Barry Goldwater in 1964 and Eugene McCarthy in 1968 fit in this category.[9] But American office seekers usually see their goal

5. David B. Truman, *The Governmental Process* (Knopf, 1951), pp. 282–83.
6. *Elections in America* (Dodd, Mead, 1968), p. 187; see also Judith H. Parris, *The Convention Problem: Issues in Reform of Presidential Nominating Procedures* (Brookings, 1972), pp. 109–14.
7. *Presidents & Promises* (CQ Press, 1985), p. 50.
8. See Everett Carll Ladd, "More Than a Dime's Worth of Difference," *Commonsense*, vol. 3 (summer 1980), pp. 51–58.
9. See Karl Hess, *In a Cause That Will Triumph: The Goldwater Campaign and the Future of Conservatism* (Doubleday, 1967), pp. 135, 157; and Eugene

as getting elected, not articulating issues. Abraham Lincoln in 1860 asked his supporters to "kindly let me be silent."[10] Franklin Roosevelt in 1932 wrote to a distressed supporter, "For heaven's sake have a little faith."[11] Issues are also badly handled by candidates because they contend for office through an adversary system that treats issues as a political football, the vehicle for scoring points; because they contend for office within a framework of two umbrella parties that blur internal disagreements in order to keep divergent factions relatively content; and because they respond to an electorate that at times is neither knowledgeable about issues nor highly politicized.

Americans' ignorance of issues is probably the most thoroughly documented tenet of voting research. In a 1964 poll 28 percent of those interviewed did not know that there was a Communist regime in China; in a 1986 poll one-third could not name the U.S. secretary of state.[12] For most people the business of earning a living and raising a family is sufficiently difficult, time-consuming, and interesting; running governments is left to those with unusual ambitions or leisure.[13] Those who most criticize

---

McCarthy, *The Year of the People* (Doubleday, 1969), pp. 84, 106, 316–17. "Education," of course, is almost always the purpose of minor-party and third-party campaigns.

10. Bruce Catton, *The Coming Fury* (Doubleday, 1961), p. 91.

11. Louis W. Koenig, *The Chief Executive* (Harcourt, Brace and World, 1964), p. 39.

12. The 1986 poll was taken in Knoxville, Tennessee, by a team from the University of Tennessee, reported in *Editor & Publisher* (January 10, 1987), p. 7. In a 1987 nationwide poll only 7 percent could name William Rehnquist as Chief Justice of the United States. See Thomas E. Patterson, "News Polls and Their Effects on Voters, Candidates and Reporters," Conference on News Polls and Presidential Selection, University of Illinois, October 8, 1987. Along the same lines, in the 1968 New Hampshire primary three out of five of those who voted for Eugene McCarthy as the Democratic nominee for president probably did not know that he was a dove on Vietnam, since they viewed the Johnson administration as not taking a hard enough line on the war. See Philip E. Converse and others, "Continuity and Change in American Politics: Parties and Issues in the 1968 Election," *American Political Science Review*, vol. 63 (December 1969), p. 1092.

13. See Peter L. Berger and Richard J. Neuhaus, *Movement and Revolution* (Doubleday, 1970), p. 16.

campaigns for their absence of reasonable policy debate are typically the most politicized; and having a consuming interest in the affairs of government (without perhaps realizing how this sets them apart), they believe that their fellow citizens should have the same passionate concerns. However, studies that stress the ignorance of the electorate on specific issues should not be interpreted as meaning that voters do not rationally sort out those issues that are of greatest concern to them. In 1960, for example, the Republican presidential candidate received 58 percent of the black vote in Atlanta; four years later, Republican Barry Goldwater, who had opposed the Civil Rights Act, received less than 1 percent of that vote.

Considering the quintessentially political and adversarial nature of campaigns, it is perhaps remarkable that issues play as large a part as they do or that voters are exposed to as much disagreement or as many precise policy commitments as they are. Though some questions (such as radical alternatives to capitalism) are taboo for the dominant parties, most major economic and social issues have been fought over at some time in some presidential campaign.

This is not to say that new policy initiatives are likely to come out of the campaign. Rarely do new issues appear, and those that have emerged generally have been modest. The Peace Corps, for example, was the only new proposal produced by the 1960 election.[14] Most issues in a campaign, by and large, are those that are already in the public arena. But besides focusing attention on existing areas of controversy, a campaign can also reflect areas of consensus. This often leads to complaints that voters are given little choice. Yet Tweedledum-Tweedledee elections mirror popular agreement on the aims of society and an acceptable pace of change. In times of real polarization, as in 1860, 1896, or the 1930s, the political process produces clear-cut alternatives.[15]

14. See Theodore C. Sorensen, *Kennedy* (Bantam, 1966), p. 205.
15. See John E. Chubb and Paul E. Peterson, "Realignment and Institutionalization" in Chubb and Peterson, eds., *The New Direction in American Politics* (Brookings, 1985), p. 1., who believe that the victories by conservative

The development of which issues a presidential campaign will focus on often grows out of an intricate interaction between candidate and electorate. Despite the ability of candidates to make their appeals without stepping outside a television studio— and to reach more people in the process—they persist in taking their cases personally to the voters. Perhaps this is why candidates have not abandoned the jet-age version of the whistle-stop, with its high cost in relation to the number of people reached. Certainly many of them must have been advised to do so. The sorts of persons who run for president may also simply find that "rubbing shoulders with the people" fills some special need. But there may be more: as former Governor Bruce Babbitt of Arizona has said, "I learn by watching the eyes of audiences."[16] A presidential candidate on the campaign trail is engaged in a process of pulse taking, seeking the voters' tolerance level, saying the same things over and over again, gauging reactions, dropping some ideas, adding others—in effect, focusing the campaign. President Kennedy in a tour of the West in September 1963— though not in a campaign contest—had just that sort of experience, according to Arthur Schlesinger, Jr.:

> He conscientiously pursued the conservation theme for several speeches. Then late on the second day, at Billings, Montana, he struck, almost by accident, a new note. Mike Mansfield was present and in his third sentence Kennedy praised the Senate leader for his part in bringing about test ban ratification. To his surprise this allusion produced strong and sustained applause. Heartened, he set forth his hope of lessening the "chance of a military collision between those two great nuclear powers which together have the power to kill 300 million people in the short space of a day." The Billings response encouraged him to make the pursuit of peace increasingly the theme of his trip.[17]

Ronald Reagan in 1980 and 1984 transformed the American political landscape "to an extent unknown since the days of Franklin Delano Roosevelt."

16. Sidney Blumenthal, "The Dawn of the New-Age Democrats," *Washington Post*, May 19, 1987. On the same point, Edmund Muskie writes, "I read faces in the crowd. Sounds are less significant, although silence is significant. . . ." *Journeys*, p. 61.

17. *A Thousand Days* (Houghton Mifflin, 1965), p. 979; also see Henry Fairlie, *The Kennedy Promise* (Doubleday, 1973), p. 65.

Kennedy went out to talk to westerners about conservation, a subject that he thought was uppermost in their minds, and discovered that they were also very concerned about something else. This was valuable information for a president.

Candidates' set speeches, often called boilerplate, though repetitious and even banal, may provide the most useful substantive basis on which voters can make their decisions. For here, in the potential presidents' own words, are what they think their campaigns are all about, the issues that they think are most serious. Unfortunately, no more than brief snippets are heard on the TV networks to illustrate some theme. News is expected to be new, and no reporter could long survive after filing a story that began, "The candidate today in Toledo said exactly the same thing he said in Seattle yesterday and in Atlanta the day before." Yet this repetition accurately reflects the campaigns. Commenting on this phenomenon after he became president, Jimmy Carter said,

> It's a strange thing that you can go through your campaign for President, and you have a basic theme that you express in a 15- or 20-minute standard speech that you give over and over and over, and the traveling press—sometimes exceeding 100 people—will never report that speech to the public. The peripheral aspects become the headlines, but the basic essence of what you stand for and what you hope to accomplish is never reported.[18]

However, in many cases the boilerplate speeches turn up on the television debates; no matter what questions the candidates are asked, they answer with excerpts from their standard stump presentations.

As the campaign progresses, the reporters are caught up in a system that forces them to report more and more marginal news (size of crowds, hecklers, staff squabbles); the candidates respond—often at the urging of special interest groups—by issuing more and more statements on marginal issues. A volume published by Nixon's campaign committee in 1968 listed his views on 227

---

18. Harvey Shapiro, "A Conversation with Jimmy Carter," *New York Times Book Review*, June 19, 1977; also see Jimmy Carter, *A Government as Good as Its People* (Simon and Schuster, 1977), p. 8.

subjects divided into 43 categories. Carter's White House staff released a 111-page compilation of the president's campaign statements that included more than 600 individual promises, goals, and general principles. A sort of Gresham's law of issues is at work: the peripheral tends to push out what is central, and nothing gets very much attention, although a great deal of information is disseminated. Surveying the media coverage of a recent campaign, James McCartney of the Knight-Ridder newspapers commented that "the public got more—of less."[19]

There is a certain irony in the belief that voters would know more if they were not told about so many things. If candidates were limited to, say, a half-dozen topics, by election day we might have a better idea of their positions on the issues they thought most important. The further irony is that to some degree it is the reporters—asking questions on the voters' behalf—who broaden the contents of a campaign beyond the limits within which information is useful for making a rational choice. But in the likely absence of any self-censorship, it is still more ironic that the voters' best interests are then served by a long (and thus boring) campaign. So much is said and reported that each citizen eventually should absorb what will be most helpful in the act of casting a ballot for a presidential candidate.

Although in some respects policy formulation in campaigns is handled better than we have the right to expect, given the nature of the system, and in some respects it is handled worse than we feel we deserve, given the seriousness of the decision we are asked to make, on one level the candidates' pledges are almost always honored, and the campaign is highly predictive. This is on the level of valence issues.[20] Some part of every campaign is conducted in symbols or code words, shorthand for social attitudes that

19. "The Triumph of Junk News," *Columbia Journalism Review* (January–February 1977), p. 19.

20. Donald Stokes makes a distinction between valence issues ("those that merely involve the linking of the parties with some condition that is positively or negatively valued by the electorate") and "position issues." See his "Spatial Models of Party Competition," in Angus Campbell and others, eds., *Elections and the Political Order* (Wiley, 1966), pp. 170–71.

cannot be easily translated into programmatic terms: *Don't Let Them Take It Away* (Democrats, 1952), *Clean Up the Mess in Washington* (Republicans, 1952), *A Choice Not an Echo* (Goldwater, 1964), *Send Them a Message* (Wallace, 1972), *Vote Republican—For a Change* (Reagan, 1980). Very few voters expect to receive a job or contract if their candidate wins, but each will receive a symbolic reward for having backed the winner. "Send them a message" is a campaign promise that is sure to be honored.

More serious is the contention that there is no real difference between candidates on issues, the Tweedledee-Tweedledum argument. But its validity depends on where one positions oneself along the ideological spectrum. Most Americans are bunched in the center, although it is a floating center and sometimes hard to locate. For those near the center, the campaign—on both programmatic and symbolic levels—functions to provide even modestly attentive voters with enough information on policy to find legitimate reasons to choose which of two candidates they would prefer to have in the White House for four years. It does not furnish an elevated level of discourse; it does not provide a carefully delineated topographical map of future public policy; and it may misdirect the voters if they are led to expect more than a politician can reasonably deliver in a system of balanced powers and in times of changeable circumstances.

Still, many of the criticisms of how issues are handled in presidential campaigns are based on esthetic rather than political judgments. Candidates bombard us with opinions in language and style and through forums that are not very elegant. The remedy, as Justice Oliver Wendell Holmes said about evils in general, may be "to grow more civilized," but this is not a matter that can be imposed by edict.

The presidential campaign also serves as a reaffirmation of our national worth. "Americans have long had a novel and overwhelming need to be reassured that they are a moral and good people," writes Michael Novak. "American soldiers give chewing gum to little children. We need to think of ourselves as good, in a manner distinctly American."[21] The campaign is part of the ritual for reasserting this sense of American goodness. Politicians tell us "what is right with America." Any candidate who endangers this ritual reaffirmation takes a chance on crossing the line between attack on policy and attack on country. This was the problem that confronted George McGovern in 1972. Public opinion polls revealed that a majority of Americans believed U.S. involvement in Vietnam was a mistake, while at the same time they saw themselves as patriotic and proud of the fact that the country "had never lost a war." In the end McGovern could not convince a substantial part of the electorate that his antiwar stance was patriotic. However, after the nation had been staggered by the back-to-back events of Vietnam and Watergate, Jimmy Carter told the voters, in effect, "This isn't your fault. It's the politicians' fault. We need a government as good and as decent as the American people." The genius of his 1976 appeal was that it offered absolution.[22]

During the presidential election year, "the nation at once celebrates and mourns itself," Garry Wills has written.[23] Yet if the celebration is what many view as a national orgy of smugness, the mourning often approaches masochism. Possibly this is a form of catharsis by which campaigns serve the public weal in providing the opportunity every fourth year to talk about all the awful things that befall society, by getting the animosities out in the open, and by purging the body politic of some of its bile. Such a restoration-by-rhetoric probably affects a very small number of voters. The rest must simply listen to predictions of the apocalypse, after which someone gets elected and the nation survives—perhaps because politicians are not as bad as other politicians say they are, perhaps because politics is not as important

21. *The Rise of the Unmeltable Ethnics* (Macmillan, 1972), p. 92.

22. See Stephen Hess, "The President: Is He the People's Choice?" in Ann Golenpaul, ed., 1977 *Information Please Almanac* (Simon and Schuster, 1976), p. 12.

23. *Nixon Agonistes* (Signet Books, 1971), p. 46.

as politicians would have us believe, perhaps because we were not listening very attentively, perhaps because of a healthy skepticism of what politicians tell us.[24]

There is a dark side to self-examination. Campaigns explicate the fears of Americans, the fear of communism or the fear of walking city streets at night. Equally the campaigns put the candidates on notice as to what the electorate most fears about them—Kennedy's Catholicism or Eisenhower's military background. Our fears may be less uplifting than our hopes, but an understanding of them is not necessarily less important to the functioning of government.

Campaigns were once full of entertainment: the torchlight parades with the marchers wearing oilskin capes to protect themselves from the dripping of the kerosene, giant outdoor rallies measured in acres, ten thousand men to the acre, handouts of E. C. Booz Old Cabin and other liquid stimulants. Whether on the frontier or in the city, nineteenth century campaigns were different from everyday life. They were colorful and tuneful. A newspaper editor recalled the 1840 Whig campaign as "a ceaseless torrent of music, still beginning, never ending."[25] The entertainment was functional, that is, it interested people in public affairs. It provided pleasant, free diversion.

"It did not detract from the intellectual content of political discourse in the 19th century that it was also designed to provide entertainment," argues Adam Yamolinksy.[26] But in the twentieth century something happened, something solemn. Perhaps, Americans may have felt, politics as entertainment is less appropriate

24. There is evidence to suggest that voters discount what they are told during campaigns. On the eve of Jimmy Carter's inauguration in 1977, one pollster, Richard Wirthlin, commented that voters are "not going to hold him to all those promises because they never believed them in the first place." See Alan L. Otten, "High Hopes, Low Expectations," *Wall Street Journal*, January 20, 1977.

25. Quoted in Freeman Cleaves, *Old Tippecanoe* (Scribner's, 1939), p. 326.

26. "Responsible Law-Making in a Technically Specialized Society," in Geoffrey C. Hazard, Jr., ed., *Law in a Changing America* (Prentice-Hall, 1968), pp. 101–02.

in a superpower than in a parochial country. And politics became very serious.

Politicians, of course, cannot compete with television entertainers. TV gives us more entertainment than we can possibly absorb. Candidates quickly learned that they can preempt popular programs only at their own peril. "Talking heads" are relegated to public TV and Sunday mornings. The candidates' commercial messages are short, unobstrusive, and in a style designed to remind us that they are using the same techniques that sell underarm deodorants.

Fortunately, however, not everyone wants to take the joy out of politics. For those who manage to stay up past the late news there are people who can still see the humor in presidential campaigns.

"Have you seen the problem he's been having?" asks Johnny Carson, September 16, 1987. His subject is Senator Joseph Biden. "He went around and made a speech and apparently he quoted— I think it was a British politician—took his speech and kind of paraphrased it as his own. And then he was charged also with taking part of Bobby Kennedy's speeches. And Biden says not to worry. He reassured his staff. He said, "'We have nothing to fear but fear itself.'"

So Biden drops out of the race and David Letterman suggests why: "He accidentally delivered Richard Nixon's resignation speech."

Thus is the functionality of entertainment in politics—making presidential campaigns more interesting to voters—left in the capable hands of late-night television comedians.

SEVEN

Candidates and Media

☆ ☆ ☆ ☆ ☆ ☆ ☆ ☆ ☆ ☆ ☆ ☆ ☆ ☆ ☆ ☆ ☆

IN 1984 "Madison Avenue brainstormers," according to Martin Schram, "worked to produce commercials to sell Ronald Reagan as skillfully as they had sold Campbell's soup, Prego spaghetti sauce, Pepsi-Cola, Gallo wine, and Yamaha motorcyles."[1] Since the 1950s, journalists, writers of fiction, and scholars have predicted repeatedly that the United States is about to experience a "neo-Orwellian revolution" that will result in "the electronic programming of the political process."[2] Frank Skeffington, the protagonist of Edwin O'Connor's *The Last Hurrah*, loses his race for mayor of Boston because he cannot adjust to the political impact of television; in *Face to Face*, a novel written by Richard Nixon's 1960 television consultant, a network executive technologically sabotages a candidate for president during a televised debate.[3] One of the best college textbooks on government warns that the "impact of television on American

1. *The Great American Video Game: Presidential Politics in the Television Age* (Morrow, 1987), pp. 224–25.
2. See Frederick G. Dutton, *Changing Sources of Power: American Politics in the 1970s* (McGraw-Hill, 1971), p. 196.
3. John G. Schneider's *The Golden Kazoo* (Rinehart, 1956) tells how an advertising campaign for a presidential candidate manipulates the voters; in Eugene Burdick's *The 480* (McGraw-Hill, 1964), the manipulation is done by computers. In both novels the manipulators work for a Republican presidential candidate, possibly reflecting the Republicans' earlier use of the new technology. Yet there is a touch of irony in the fact that Burdick's novel clearly was modeled on work done for John F. Kennedy. See Ithiel de Sola Pool, Robert P. Abelson, and Samuel L. Popkin, *Candidates, Issues, and Strategies: A Computer Simulation of the 1960 and 1964 Presidential Elections* (MIT Press, 1964).

politics since 1952 should not be underestimated."[4] Judging from the literature, this has never been a problem.[5]

Neither should it be overestimated. Former New York City Mayor John Lindsay, perhaps the most telegenic candidate ever to seek a presidential nomination, and one who used television extensively in his 1972 campaign, was ignominiously defeated in all the primaries he entered. Richard Nixon, possibly the least telegenic candidate, carried forty-nine states in winning a second presidential term that year. The most infamous commercial in a presidential contest, the "Daisy Girl" spot made for Lyndon Johnson in 1964, was shown only once, and if everyone who saw it had voted for Barry Goldwater, the election would still have gone to Johnson.[6]

The reach of television is considerable, of course. Almost every home has at least one set, and most Americans judge it their main source of news.[7] But as paid media—that is, as a commercial enterprise selling airtime to candidates to sell themselves to the voters—television has never caused the nomination of a presidential candidate or the election of a presidential nominee.

The expectation that presidential candidates can be sold like breakfast food rests on three assumptions: (a) media manipulators know how to sell candidates as they apparently know how to sell

4. Milton C. Cummings, Jr., and David Wise, *Democracy Under Pressure* (Harcourt Brace Jovanovich, 1971), p. 298.

5. Also see Vance Packard, *The Hidden Persuaders* (McKay, 1957); Joe McGinniss, *The Selling of the President 1968* (Trident, 1969); and Dean Alger, "Television Perceptions of Reality and the Presidential Election of '84," *PS* (Winter 1987), pp. 49–57.

6. The commercial was run during NBC's "Monday Night at the Movies" on September 7, 1964. It showed a little girl plucking daisy petals while a doomsday voice began a countdown, followed by a mushroom cloud and the voice of President Johnson reminding listeners that "these are the stakes." See Theodore H. White, *The Making of the President 1964* (Atheneum, 1965), p. 322.

7. For a skeptical assessment of what viewers learn from TV news, see John P. Robinson and Mark R. Levy, *The Main Source* (Sage, 1986); for another view, see Merrill McLoughlin and others, "Television's Blinding Power," *U.S. News & World Report* (July 27, 1987), pp. 18–21.

breakfast food; (b) voters are as willing to swallow a sales pitch for a candidate as they apparently are for a breakfast food; and (c) candidates are willing to be sold like breakfast food. All are dubious propositions.

The advertising profession has had "few inhibitions against the propagation of myths that inflated its own capabilities," said V. O. Key.[8] Many grandiose claims are little more than self-advertisements by those seeking political clients. Initially presidential candidates did employ commercial advertising agencies, and the early advertisements, as Stanley Kelley's analysis of the 1952 Eisenhower-Stevenson contest illustrates, are not very different from attempts to sell breakfast food.[9] Today, however, the advertising agencies of limited political instinct have been largely replaced by media consultants who specialize in politics or by ad hoc advertising agencies put together by candidates for the sole purpose of producing their media campaigns. This new breed of expert is somewhat more restrained in claims for the selling power of television, perhaps because research has shown that viewers "pay attention primarily to content that already interests them and that is congenial to their point of view." And according to Harold Mendelsohn and Irving Crespi, "The injection of high doses of political information during the frenetic periods of national campaigns does very little to alter the deeply rooted, tightly held political attitudes (or prejudices) of most voters."[10] Advertising could not save six Republican senators in

8. *Public Opinion and American Democracy* (Knopf, 1961), p. 6.

9. *Professional Public Relations and Political Power* (Johns Hopkins University Press, 1956), p. 189. Example of a 1952 commercial: VOICE : "Mr. Eisenhower, what about the high cost of living?" EISENHOWER: "My wife, Mamie, worries about the same thing. I tell her it's our job to change that on November 4."

10. Kurt Lang and Gladys Engle Lang, *Politics and Television* (Quadrangle, 1968), p. 16; and Mendelsohn and Crespi, *Polls, Television, and the New Politics* (Chandler, 1970), p. 248. According to Andrew Rosenthal, "Madison Avenue Comes Back to Politics," *New York Times*, October 9, 1987, among commercial advertising agencies there is a trend back into political campaigns. While once they saw politics as low paying and capable of alienating important clients, "some advertising executives now say political work can be a boon. They point to Saatchi & Saatchi, a British company whose rapid expansion is sometimes linked to the

1986 who outspent their opponents by an average of 75 percent and still lost their seats.[11]

Each side has its own media manipulators, theoretically canceling the actions of the other side's. Campaign consultants do not lack theories about which techniques work and which ones do not, but in the absence of hard facts to substantiate competing claims, they tend to promote those approaches that they think were successful in the previous election.

Yet voters remain remarkably resistant to the sales pitch. At a time when more than half of all Americans of college age enter college, voters are less likely prospects to be indoctrinated, manipulated, or subliminally influenced in their choice of presidents. They know when they are seeing a commercial, and they adjust accordingly. "Viewers see through the 'artful' staging of media events. . . . [They] may watch more and more television, but they believe less and less," writes Edwin Diamond.[12]

Also overlooked sometimes is the resistance of candidates to being merchandised and sold.[13] Candidates do spend immense

---

worldwide exposure it received from political advertising for Prime Minister Margaret Thatcher."

11. See Robert J. Samuelson, "Why the Campaign 'Reform' Effort Is a Fraud," *Washington Post*, July 8, 1987. Television and radio time costs $73.4 million, or 38.9 percent of the amount spent on 1986 Senate races, according to a study sponsored by the National Association of Broadcasters. See Andrew Rosenthal, "On the Air: $97 Million Spent in '86," *New York Times*, July 14, 1987.

12. "The Myth of Media Power," *Skeptic* (September–October 1976), p. 38.

13. Nelson Rockefeller during the crucial 1964 California primary and Barry Goldwater in that fall's campaign canceled television presentations of films that their staffs had produced because they found them to be in questionable taste and not in the public interest. For an account of the Goldwater film, see Karl Hess, *In a Cause That Will Triumph: The Goldwater Campaign and the Future of Conservatism* (Doubleday, 1967), p. 140; and Stephen Shadegg, *What Happened to Goldwater?* (Holt, Rinehart and Winston, 1965), pp. 254–55. For an account of the Rockefeller film, see Gene Wyckoff, *The Image Candidates* (Macmillan, 1968), pp. 179–87. Although Joe McGinnis in *The Selling of the President 1968* stressed the guile of advertising men in trying to package Nixon, an underlying theme is that "Nixon had never liked the idea of advertising men giving him an image" (p. 81). The same point is made by John Osborne, "Nixon Through the

sums on television, of course, and do make adjustments in their presentations and schedules. (They plan and time visual events so as to increase their chances of being seen on the evening news, for example.) But the typical barnstorming campaign—despite increased risks of assassination—suggests that improved transportation technology affects the candidates' uses of their own time more than does improved communications technology. An explanation would have to take into account the deeply ingrained tribal rituals in political campaigning. All presidents to date grew up in a nontelevision society. Future generations of candidates will be more attuned to television's potential. Yet William Jennings Bryan, the inventor of the whistle-stop campaign, profoundly influenced politicians who could never have seen him and are undoubtedly not aware of his effect on how they run for office; in short, they are part of a continuum of political behavior in which fundamental changes come gradually.

The sheer chaos of the presidential selection process also acts as a powerful check against manipulation through the media. The candidates propose themselves, build their own organizations to secure their nominations, raise funds, are not anointed by their parties until late in the season, and, during the period of maximum voter interest, compete for attention with thousands of claimants for lesser elective positions. The permanent party organizations are weak and cannot support candidates (other than an incumbent) before the conventions. There is a very high turnover of players every four years—candidates, staff, experts. Even experienced politicians generally are novices at running for president. An advertising campaign for a commercial product is based on long-range planning and allocation of resources, continuity, and recognition of the brand name. But these factors hardly exist in U.S. presidential election politics. (The theoretical risk of manipulation is greater in Great Britain, where there are strong permanent party organizations with a capacity for contin-

Tube," in *The First Two Years of the Nixon Watch: The First Year* (Liveright, 1971), pp. 105–08.

uous selling campaigns, and voters select between the equivalent of brand names, Tory and Labour.)

A principal effect of television on presidential selection politics is, however, its ability to build name recognition and create instant celebrities. Being "Jimmy Who?" from Plains, Georgia, worked to Carter's advantage in early 1976, adding a sense of mystery to his candidacy. Gary Hart's name recognition among Democrats in 1984, less than 50 percent at the beginning of the year, jumped to nearly 100 percent by "Super Tuesday," March 13.[14] Filmmaker Charles Guggenheim notes, "There's a phenomenon in American politics [in state primaries] which television has emphasized: men who have no record are often more appealing than men who have a record. . . . TV dramatizes this political virginity. Before there was television, an unknown couldn't run at all because he couldn't get the exposure. With television, he can become known in a very short time."[15] The technology exists to make it easier for a little-known politician or a nonpolitician (who is well financed) to accumulate respectable showings in early presidential primaries. But the nonpolitician probably would have to have a credible distinction, perhaps in some form of public service. Thus television has the latent capacity to increase the number of people seeking presidential nominations.

Even if three decades of experience with television in presidential elections has proved less hazardous to the health of the body politic than early forecasts suggested, TV's potential for manipulation is the sort of concern that deserves constant attention. Some have proposed that broadcasters ban all political advertising of less than five minutes, all film clips and recordings of candidates unless the opposition candidates have the opportunity to reply simultaneously, all dramatizations of political issues, all disparaging attacks on a candidate unless made by the opposing candidate, and all new material during the last forty-

14. See Paul R. Abramson, John H. Aldrich, and David W. Rohde, *Change and Continuity in the 1984 Elections* (CQ Press, 1986), p. 23.

15. Quoted in Lewis W. Wolfson, "The Media Masters," *Washington Post*, February 20, 1972.

eight hours of the campaign.[16] But while these proposals are aimed at promoting a more rational discussion of issues, free of gimmicks and mudslinging, they might not achieve this objective, as the following example illustrates.

A 1972 commercial opens with the camera on a formation of toy soldiers. "The McGovern defense plan," says the narrator. "He would cut the Marines by one-third. The Air Force by one-third. He'd cut Navy personnel by one-fourth. He would cut interceptor planes by one-half. The Navy fleet by one-half. . . ." A hand comes across the screen and sweeps away the toys. "President Nixon doesn't believe we should play games with our national security," concludes the narrator.[17] This commercial is disparaging and a dramatization and is presented in less than five minutes. Yet is it unfair? The size of the defense force is a legitimate issue, and the differences between the candidates were notable: McGovern, although hardly playing games, did propose precise budget cuts, which could be translated into terms of reductions in personnel and equipment.

The "McGovern defense plan" commercial is a so-called negative spot, a type of advertising that some people find especially objectionable. Their objections imply that the only information voters should have to help them make rational decisions is positive. Clearly not so. Also, whether a candidate can present a useful message in a minute or less is not the open-and-shut case that opponents of spot commercials have made of it. Spot commercials have been attacked as oversimplifications and distortions.[18] Distortion, however, is not inherent in the technique;

16. Paul A. Porter, "Did You Know Ronald Reagan Shot Lincoln?" *Washington Post*, January 23, 1972. For other proposals to counter negative advertising, see Bob Davis, "Lawmakers Move to Curb Negative Ads, Calling Them 'Punk Political' Attacks That Stir Cynicism," *Wall Street Journal*, June 9, 1987.

17. See Thomas E. Patterson and Robert D. McClure, *Political Advertising: Voter Reaction to Televised Political Commercials* (Princeton, N.J.: Citizens' Research Foundation, 1974), p. 15.

18. See Alan L. Otten, "Out, Damned Spot," *Wall Street Journal*, March 9, 1972; and Warren Weaver, Jr., "Call It Fast Food for Thought," *New York Times*, August 8, 1987.

there can be thirty-minute distortions. All that a spot is, is short, as are most items on network news programs. Candidates can state important positions in a very few seconds ("I favor X"); what they cannot do is explain them thoroughly. A commercial of any length, unlike a news broadcast, is the sponsor's attempt to tell one side of the story. Like all commercial elements of the campaign that candidates control—billboards, bumper stickers, fliers, and direct mail as well as media advertising—it is part of a simplification process. Trying to reach a mass audience through mass tools leaves little room for subtlety, but it does not necessarily mean that candidates are incapable of higher thoughts.

With the exception of Republican dirty tricks in 1972, which did not involve media manipulation, the more prominent the office sought, the less likely that mud will be slung.[19] Unethical appeals were notably absent from the campaigns of Ford, Carter, Reagan, and Mondale. Yet, clean or dirty, the style of the campaign does not profoundly affect the style of the presidency. Candidates sometimes act as clowns; presidents do not.

The media give presidents a considerable advantage when they run for reelection. This is especially true of network TV. "Television news loves the presidency," according to Michael J. Robinson and Margaret A. Sheehan. "It may not like the incumbent; it may not like any incumbent, but the office of the president has become the *sine qua non* of network journalism."[20] While not all presidents know how to make the most effective use of the media, Steven R. Weisman, who was the White House correspondent for the *New York Times* during Reagan's first term, believes that the president he covered "achieved a new level of

19. For "dirty tricks" in nineteenth century presidential campaigns, see Eugene H. Roseboom, *A History of Presidential Elections* (Macmillan, 1957), pp. 90–91, 132–33, 270, 282–83. Paul E. Peterson argues that negative campaigning dominates in periods "when major issues are not open to dispute," and, therefore, may be a reflection of "a healthy, not a degenerate, body politic." See "Mudslinging Thrives Because Top Issues Aren't in Dispute," *Los Angeles Times*, November 4, 1986.

20. *Over the Wire and on TV: CBS and UPI in Campaign '80* (Russell Sage Foundation, 1983), p. 191.

control over the mechanics of modern communication."[21] Presidents ask for, and usually receive, all the network TV and radio time they desire. Reagan chose not to hold many press conferences; instead he read a radio address to the nation every Saturday, which was then reported in the fat Sunday newspapers. Still, it was Franklin Roosevelt, another great communicator, who said, "People tire of seeing the same name day after day in the important headlines of the papers, and the same voice night after night over the radio. . . . Individual psychology cannot, because of human weakness, be attuned for long periods of time to a constant repetition of the highest note in the scale."[22]

Newsmakers have always accused newsgatherers of bias. A generation of Democratic candidates—Franklin Roosevelt through Adlai Stevenson—thought that the press was a bastion of conservatism. Since Spiro Agnew's famous speeches of 1969 the press is usually attacked as being too liberal.[23] Survey research has shown that most journalists, especially in Washington, classify themselves as liberals or have voted for the Democrat in recent presidential elections.[24] Strangely, however, the candidates whose prospects seem to have been most adversely effected by media coverage—Ted Kennedy when running for his party's nomination in 1980, Jimmy Carter's reelection campaign, John Glenn's efforts in 1984, and, of course, Gary Hart and Joseph Biden in 1987—have all been Democrats.[25]

21. "The President and the Press," *New York Times Magazine* (October 14, 1984), p. 34. For a discussion of White House problems with the press during the Carter presidency, see Lloyd N. Cutler, "Foreign Policy on Deadline," *Foreign Policy*, no. 56 (Fall 1984), pp. 113–28.

22. Quoted in Arthur M. Schlesinger, Jr., *The Politics of Upheaval* (Sentry Books, 1966), pp. 9–10. Also see James Keogh, *President Nixon and the Press* (Funk and Wagnalls, 1971), p. 39.

23. Agnew's attack on TV came in a November 13, 1969, speech to the Midwest Regional Republican Committee meeting in Des Moines, Iowa; he extended his criticism to newspapers on November 20, 1969, in an address to the Montgomery, Alabama, Chamber of Commerce.

24. See Stephen Hess, *The Washington Reporters* (Brookings, 1981), pp. 87–88; also see S. Robert Lichter, Stanley Rothman, and Linda S. Lichter, *The Media Elite* (Adler and Adler, 1986).

25. See Michael J. Robinson, "Where's the Beef? Media and Media Elites

Television makes escaping from politics more and more difficult for Americans. But social scientists have found it extremely difficult to measure TV's influence on presidential campaigns, although others argue that so much TV must have consequences.[26] Still, at this time there is no evidence that free media—presenting news and other public service programs on TV—have caused the nomination or election of a single candidate.[27]

While some contend that the televised debates of 1960 and 1976 elected John Kennedy and Jimmy Carter, those elections were so close that any single factor—including debates—could have been said to have made the difference.[28] TV debates are now part of the political landscape, however, and according to James M. Perry of the *Wall Street Journal*, 1988 "is sure to be the greatest debating campaign in history."[29] Democratic candidates held a debate among themselves on July 1, 1987, more than a year before their national convention, and by late summer there were nearly three dozen debates scheduled. Nelson Polsby, a leading political scientist, worries about this development. "Debates are a test of peripheral skills, clearly not trivial ones,

in 1984," in Austin Ranney, ed., *The American Elections of 1984* (Duke University Press, 1985), p. 178.

26. See Reuven Frank, a former president of NBC News, quoted in Edward Jay Epstein, *News from Nowhere* (Vintage, 1974), p. 9. It could be claimed, of course, that it was the televising of Nixon's "Checkers" speech that kept him on the Republican ticket in 1952; this assumes that his case would have fallen short if he had used other means of communicating. See Mark Shields, "A Lesson That Hart Learned," *Washington Post*, September 15, 1987.

27. See Thomas E. Patterson and Robert D. McClure, *The Unseeing Eye: The Myth of Television Power in National Politics* (Putnam, 1976); and Jeff Greenfield, *The Real Campaign* (Summit Books, 1982).

28. See Pierre Salinger, *With Kennedy* (Doubleday, 1966), p. 47. Marshall McLuhan considered the contents of the 1960 debates irrelevant but judged them decisive in terms of image. He speaks of "the shy young sheriff" (Kennedy) and "the railroad lawyer" (Nixon) in *Understanding Media* (McGraw-Hill, 1964), p. 330. For an opposing view, see Samuel Lubell, "Personalities vs. Issues," in Sidney Kraus, ed., *The Great Debates* (Peter Smith, 1968), p. 160.

29. "Never Before Have So Very Many Been Ready to Debate So Very Much to Be Elected President," *Wall Street Journal*, June 22, 1987.

but not the skills central to whether someone has the wisdom and ability to govern well."[30] But debates do give more Americans than ever before a greater opportunity to learn more about those who would be president. This is probably the most positive thing to come out of the age of television.

If television's impact on voting behavior has been less than many observers expected, part of the reason lies in the commercial nature of the medium. Entertainment will always be the dominant fare. This is where the networks and stations make their money, and this sets the tone for news programming.[31] TV's level of analysis, choice of subject matter, tolerance of deviant opinion (affiliated stations have the right to reject network programming), and willingness to take sides on issues are all affected by the medium's effort to appeal to a broad audience.

The format of news programs contributes to mass appeal but not to an enlightened citizenry. The average story is seen for a hundred seconds, and there is a subtle preference for news that focuses on action rather than ideas. As Ted Koppel has said, "There is not much room on television for complexity."[32] Television tells stories essentially through pictures. A fire or a riot can be easily visualized; it is more difficult to present simply and quickly a moving picture of impoundment or executive privilege.[33]

30. Quoted in Frank Clifford, "'88 Race? It's Highly Debatable," *Los Angeles Times*, July 25, 1987. Also see Nelson W. Polsby, "Debatable Thoughts on Presidential Debates," in Austin Ranney, ed., *The Past and Future of Presidential Debates* (American Enterprise Institute, 1979), pp. 175–86.

31. In August 1987 the Federal Communications Commission repealed the so-called fairness doctrine, which required broadcasters to give contrasting views on important public issues; the immediate reaction of most experts, however, was that this would have little effect on what is aired. See Charlotte Grimes, "Fairness on the Air," *St. Louis Post-Dispatch*, August 6, 1987.

32. "The Vannatizing of America," *Duke*, vol. 73 (July-August 1987), p. 36.

33. Sir Kenneth Clark wrote of his famous BBC series, "Civilisation," that it scanted the subjects of law and philosophy because he "could not think of any way of making them visually interesting." Quoted in Richard W. Jencks, "A Picture Isn't Always Worth a Thousand Words on TV," *Wall Street Journal*, August 20, 1987.

Moreover, the constantly moving pictures—image following image as on a conveyor belt—does not allow thinking time or learning time. Even if a profound thought is presented, the picture cannot be stopped to give the listener an opportunity to absorb its significance. The technology of television, particularly editing, has created a new concept of time. Television time, like a Mack Sennett chase, is a speeded-up version of reality, a concentration of data that does away with the repetition and pause of human communications. It is the viewers' expectations of things happening in television time that can make the interview program so painfully dull. Thoughtful political discourse will always be too slow-moving to compete on commercial television time.

If the people increasingly get their headlines from the twelve-items-in-twenty-three-minutes format of the evening news on network television and presidents continue to go over the heads of the news media, what role does this leave for the daily newspapers? The better papers are moving toward more interpretive reporting and away from the who-what-where-when-how journalism that has been the staple of newsgathering in the United States. Such pacesetting publications as the *Washington Post, New York Times, Wall Street Journal*, and *Los Angeles Times* make highly intelligent use of public opinion surveys, arrange seminar-sized focus groups to observe elections from the vantage points of the voters, cover the candidates' television commercials as news, and assign groups of reporters to assess a topic from various angles. The print media cannot compete with radio and TV in terms of being first to report fast-breaking events. The newspapers' advantage is the ability to devote more space and time to a story. The pattern, says the *Wall Street Journal's* Albert R. Hunt, is for "newspapers to set the media agenda of campaign coverage, especially in the initial phase." He notes that virtually all the major stories in 1984 started with print journalists and were then taken over by television.[34]

34. See "The Media and Presidential Campaigns," in A. James Reichley, ed., *Elections American Style* (Brookings, 1987), p. 58.

Columnists and national political reporters have a unique role in presidential election politics that has almost nothing to do with the general public. As the selection process has become more diffuse, some journalists have assumed a function once assigned to traditional political brokers, the party bosses. At the simplest level these journalists act as the connective link between politicians, passing along messages that once might have been communicated in smoke-filled rooms. When Richard Nixon wished to cue the political community that he was considering Spiro Agnew for vice president in 1968, he planted the story with David S. Broder of the *Washington Post*. When George McGovern wished to suggest that his running mate, Thomas Eagleton, should get off the ticket, he gave a not-for-attribution interview to Jules Witcover of the *Los Angeles Times*.[35]

Political reporters also act as talent scouts, a prerogative that belonged almost exclusively to politicians in the nineteenth century.[36] In addition to informing the public on the activities of the presidential contenders, they tell the politicians who should be considered for the presidency. The candidacy of Wendell Willkie is a prime example of the press's contribution in expanding the talent pool. Journalists also may narrow the talent pool if they repel potential contenders who are unwilling to expose their private lives to the media's scrutiny; this, however, is easier to claim than to prove.

Journalists play a large part in devising the rules by which the contenders are rated, both by the public and by politicians. They determined, for example, that good showings in New Hampshire by McCarthy in 1968 and McGovern in 1972 were "triumphs," whereas the winners of those primaries (Johnson and Muskie,

---

35. Timothy Crouse, "The Boys on the Bus," *Rolling Stone* (October 12, 1972), pp. 54, 56, 58. See also Richard Dougherty, *Goodbye, Mr. Christian: A Personal Account of McGovern's Rise and Fall* (Doubleday, 1973), pp. 197–98.

36. See David S. Broder, "Political Reporters in Presidential Politics," in Charles Peters and Timothy J. Adams, eds., *Inside the System* (Praeger, 1970), esp. pp. 11–15. Broder also points out that the press serves as "summarizer of the candidate's positions," "race caller or handicapper," "public defender," and sometimes "unpaid assistant campaign manager."

respectively) were awarded "setbacks."[37] Politicians try to influence the reporters' interpretations, but generally they accept the press as the final arbiter. Thus the power of the press grows in direct proportion to the proliferation of state primaries.

Finally, columnists act as political advisers to the contenders. Their opinions can be read by anyone who buys a newspaper, yet the contents suggest that they are often interested in a more limited audience. Martin F. Nolan of the *Boston Globe* has written, "Many—though by no means all—syndicated columnists now fill the frankly partisan role that minor newspapers held in the early days of the republic. They are mouthpieces for ideological factions in a party, originally dependent for their sources and prestige on chumminess with or employment under a major political figure."[38] The popularity of the late Theodore White's series on *The Making of the President* (1960–72) has caused the public to become more aware of the preconvention jockeying and the press more anxious to join in the process.[39]

So the press has become an integral part of the presidential selection process, moving from the sidelines to the playing fields. Important newspaper journalists, whose words are read regularly in Washington and New York, are now more influential than the average governor or senator—not because they reach masses of people, but because within the political community they are looked to as rules makers, talent scouts, advisers, and whistle-blowers. Television correspondents and the anchors of network

37. In 1968 New Hampshire Democrats gave Johnson 50 percent and McCarthy 42 percent; the 1972 results were Muskie 46 percent, McGovern 37 percent. See Peter M. Yu, "By the Numbers: A Statistical Profile of New Hampshire," in Gary R. Orren and Nelson W. Polsby, eds., *Media and Momentum* (Chatham House, 1987), p. 191.

38. "Faust at the Racetrack: Let the Reader Beware," in Frederick Dutton, ed., *Playboy's Election Guide*, 1972 (Playboy Press, 1972), p. 129.

39. James M. Perry severely criticizes his colleagues for their coverage of the campaigns: "We have become nitpickers, peeking into dusty corners, looking for the squabbles, celebrating the trivia, and leaping to those sweeping, cosmic, melodramatic conclusions and generalities that mark the Teddy White view of American politics." See *Us and Them: How the Press Covered the 1972 Election* (Clarkson N. Potter, 1973), pp. 9–10.

news programs, although better known to the public, play a more passive preconvention role, given the characteristics of their medium, and then become more important during the general election when numbers replace elites as the name of the game.

Even the contours of the presidential campaign are shaped in part by the wishes of the press corps. While national political reporters may cloak themselves in professional cynicism, they greet the coming of the first primary in New Hampshire the way children anxiously await the arrival of the circus in town. As Mark Shields has written, "The media like New Hampshire because it's manageable and fun. . . . It's a great place, small enough to run into old friends and to share a cup of cheer at the hotel bar."[40] Thus this primary is always reported out of all proportion to the number of convention delegates at stake. In 1984, for instance, "the New Hampshire primary received more attention [from ABC, CBS, NBC, and the *New York Times*] than was given all the contests for delegates in the 17 southern and border states (including Texas and Florida) and the 7 Rocky Mountain states combined."[41] What also happens, as David Broder, Richard Reeves, and others have pointed out, is that reporters become bored by the repetition of a campaign at just the time that voters are tuning into presidential politics. They then focus on insider news instead of the more basic information that voters need.[42]

The modern presidential campaign was invented in 1896 by Marcus Alonzo Hanna, the Republican national chairman, and William Jennings Bryan, the Democratic candidate. Hanna ended the chaos of fund-raising by levying regular assessments on the

40. "The Most Important Primary State," *Washington Post*, September 4, 1987.

41. William S. Adams, "As New Hampshire Goes . . . " in Gary R. Orren and Nelson W. Polsby, eds., *Media and Momentum* (Chatham House, 1987), p. 42.

42. Broder writes, "It's another example of our serving the clique of insiders rather than the broad mass of our readers and viewers." See his *Behind the Front Page* (Simon and Schuster, 1987), p. 263.

financial community. He recruited, trained, and scheduled 1,400 party orators, devising a system of surrogate candidates who took to the hustings in place of William McKinley. He assigned speakers to trail Bryan as a sort of Republican truth squad. Hanna's Bureau of Publications distributed 120 million pieces of literature in thirteen languages, including Hebrew; press releases and mats were sent to county newspapers with a combined circulation of 5 million. Hanna divided the electorate into voting blocs, assigning a staff and a budget to each, so that within the Republican National Committee there were operations specifically directed at women (who had been given the vote in Colorado, Wyoming, and Utah), blacks, Germans, traveling salesmen, even bicyclists. Through competitive bidding, central purchasing, and strict audits, he trimmed the waste factor by half. Key states were polled repeatedly to determine changes in public opinion, and what the pollsters missed was undoubtedly picked up by Hanna's spies at Democratic headquarters. At the same time, Bryan took his cause directly to the voters, traveling across the country in a railroad car misnamed "The Idler." He averaged 80,000 words spoken daily, and by election day he figured he had logged over 18,000 miles, delivering some 600 speeches to 5 million people in 27 states.[43]

Since then, there have been tremendous changes in communications technology. Changes, however, have been absorbed into the basic format that Hanna and Bryan invented. The campaign *looks* different—as airplanes and railroad trains look different—but newer technology has not altered the nature of politicians or of their appeals to the electorate. Reaching voters through television rather than through a megaphone has not created a neo-Orwellian revolution. There is nothing comparable in politics to the sea change that the cubists brought to painting, or literature before and after Joyce and Proust. What we have in politics are largely variations on a theme. Mark Hanna in 1984 would have been perfectly at home as Ronald Reagan's campaign manager.

43. See Stephen Hess, "The Making of the President, 1896," in *The Nineties* (American Heritage, 1967), pp. 30–35, 130–38.

EIGHT Candidates and Parties

☆ ☆ ☆ ☆ ☆ ☆ ☆ ☆ ☆ ☆ ☆ ☆ ☆ ☆ ☆ ☆

A PRESIDENTIAL nomination in the United States is not the final reward for service to a political party that it is in parliamentary democracies. American parties can reject a Robert Taft and choose a Dwight Eisenhower, as the Republicans did in 1952, casting aside the party's Senate leader for a candidate of such unsure affiliation that he had been urged to run as a Democrat four years earlier. Rarely have parties confused the prospects of winning the presidency with long loyalty to their cause. In fact, outsiders may have an advantage because they accumulate fewer enemies. As the outsider in 1976, Jimmy Carter seemed to be running against both the Republicans and his own party, or at least against congressional Democrats.

At the same time, candidates often ignore their parties. In seeking presidential nominations, they build personal organizations composed of people whose basic allegiance is to them rather than to the party. They start with a small coterie of those who work for them or advise them in government—friends and family—then expand to include experts, such as advertising executives and pollsters, and finally pick up foot soldiers, often young people attracted by their personality or their chances of winning. American candidates traditionally are on their own until the convention decides who will be the party's choice.

The situation was not always thus. When Franklin Roosevelt became a contender for the 1932 Democratic nomination, his campaign manager went around the country drumming up support among state party leaders. Today a candidate probably will move first to capture the interest of a handful of leading journalists, whom collectively Russell Baker calls "the Great Mentioner," that is, "the source of self-fulfilling stories that a person has been 'mentioned' as a possible presidential nominee."[1] Candidates once bargained with powerful state party leaders for delegates, either before or during the convention, just as they relied heavily on such leaders to help carry their states in the November election. Even if successful nominees were not particularly indebted to their national parties, they emerged from the campaign with binding ties to a collection of state and local parties. But now that direct primaries have replaced caucuses as the means of picking convention delegates, it is no longer sufficient to have the support of local party leaders, although as long as they can deliver the vote they have to be reckoned with.

Once the local parties started to decline, they had nothing—such as control over candidate selection—to brake their slide. Public discontent after the 1968 Democratic convention, followed by changes in party rules, has encouraged the proliferation of primaries. At the same time, the end of winner-take-all primaries on the Democratic side increases the potential for factionalism within state parties and hastens their decline. Public funding of presidential campaigns since 1976 lessens the fund-raising role of the parties. The candidates now have the means of communication to reach voters directly. Television commercials can replace doorbell ringers. Political consultants can provide the candidates with services they once received from the parties.

Gone is the brokered convention, in which a small group of kingmakers could choose Warren G. Harding in a smoke-filled room. Gone too is the favorite son candidate—governors or senators who tried to hold their state delegations as bargaining chips at a national convention or who merely sought a moment of glory. The Democratic rules changes in 1972 were "designed frankly to eliminate the sometimes entertaining 'favorite son'

1. William R. Keech and Donald R. Matthews, *The Party's Choice* (Brookings, 1976), p. 13. Also see Theodore J. Lowi, *The Personal President* (Cornell University Press, 1985), pp. 67–96.

nominating speech."[2] Soon these political terms will sound as archaic as sending a candidate "up the salt river," which is how an election defeat was described in the nineteenth century.

In waging the general election campaign the candidate's organization now becomes the party organization, not the other way around. This is especially true for candidates of the minority party. As Richard Nixon said in 1960, "I'm not going to ask anybody here to vote on November the 8th because of the party label that I happen to wear."[3] After the election the president-elect and a small group of advisers plan the impending administration far from the party's national committee. The new president chooses a national chairman but, like the son who goes to sea, the new chairman may never be heard from again. The national committee has little to offer the president; it is just another supplicant for presidential favors.

A president does not repudiate the party's platform. But neither can the platform be said to set an administration's agenda, which is more the product of campaign speeches, the ideas of appointees, and circumstances as they arise. Job seekers grumble that party work is not given any special reward when an administration is staffed. And relatively few members of each administration eventually go back to their states to help build the parties.

This growing irrelevance of parties has consequences. Some contend that it widens the gap between the White House and Congress.[4] Others see the future in stark terms. "The ultimate cost of the decline of parties is the loss of popular control over public policies," according to Gerald M. Pomper. "If the decline of partisan politics continues . . . the loss will be that of

2. *Call to Order, A Report by the Commission on Rules* (Democratic National Committee, 1972), p. 56.

3. *Freedom of Communication*, Part 2: *The Speeches of Vice President Richard M. Nixon*, S. Rept. 994, 87 Cong. 1 sess. (GPO, 1961), pt. 2, pp. 81–82.

4. Xandra Kayden, "Report on Campaign Finance, Based on the Experiences of the 1976 Presidential Campaigns," unpublished paper (Institute of Politics, Harvard University, 1977), p. 50.

democracy."[5] The events in the 1972 presidential election campaign that collectively became known as Watergate provide a sorrowful reminder of how much we miss by not having a strong two-party system with a professional code of ethics for those who participate in the political process. Even if Watergate is viewed merely as a failure of men, it may be that politics can cause people to act more immorally than they might in other pursuits. There is no reason to believe, for example, that the bright young men who appeared before the Ervin Committee in 1973 were not good husbands or good parents, or that in most matters they failed to conduct themselves in an exemplary manner. Jerry Bruno, a Democratic politician associated with the Kennedys, once wrote, "When you're part of a political campaign, the stakes are as high as they come. . . . I think sometimes it's what fighting a war or playing a pro football game is like."[6] The analogies are apt. Modern warfare is often a suspension of morality, often in the name of morality; professional football is a sport in which infractions of the rules are penalized by loss of yards but rarely by banishment, so that breaking the rules becomes a calculated risk, not an act of depravity.

The ad hoc staffing arrangements of presidential campaigns may also remove the participants temporarily from the worlds in which they individually abide by the codes of conduct of whatever occupations engage them. There are some people who leave their morality at home when they enter a presidential campaign. Members of a candidate's campaign staff see the world of politics as different, less enduring than the "real world," and for some this makes a difference in their conduct. Many of the people who work in presidential campaigns are amateurs in that politics is not their profession, though they may have varying degrees of political experience. This raises questions about individual and group ethics in an election system that lacks a professional

5. "The Decline of the Party in American Elections," *Political Science Quarterly*, vol. 92 (Spring 1977), p. 41.
6. Jerry Bruno and Jeff Greenfield, *The Advance Man* (Morrow, 1971), p. 29.

memory. Professionalism, by definition, includes a set of standards by which individuals are judged and on which their status depends. High standards of conduct are strengthened by, if not dependent on, continuing relationships. Yet continuity is exactly what is absent from the organization of presidential campaigns, and continuity is exactly what the parties are all about.

Running presidential campaigns under the centralized control of the parties would not produce the millennium. Parties, after all, brought us Warren Harding as well as Woodrow Wilson. But parties did not bring us Watergate. It is highly unlikely that the Republican National Committee would seriously consider breaking into the offices of the Democratic National Committee, or vice versa, if only, as David S. Broder contends, because "our political parties are old, and they expect to be in business a long time. Neither of them has any great temptation to kick down the walls, or to pursue tactics when temporarily in power that will invite revenge from the opposition when it (inevitably) returns to power."[7]

Broder does not mean to sanitize political parties. The corruption of party machines was the motor force of the reform movement that started a century ago. But recent scandals—at least on the national level—are not associated with party, although this may be true only because the parties now have so little opportunity to create trouble.

It is doubtful that American political parties can ever regain the influence they had in the nineteenth century. Government has replaced them as dispenser of social services, patronage is no longer an attractive lure to recruit political workers, a permanent career service now fills all but the top jobs in government, different forms of entertainment and voluntary associations compete with the parties on unequal terms, and television gives the voters increased possibilities to get information and judge can-

7. *The Party's Over* (Harper and Row, 1972), p. 179. Also see Broder's "Two True Professionals . . . Muskie and [Howard] Baker Treat Today's Adversaries with Respect, Because They Know They May Be Tomorrow's Allies," *Washington Post*, March 3, 1987.

didates outside the party context. The social composition of the country has also changed. Yesterday's wave of immigrants—Irish, Italians, Jews—once looked to the parties as part of the Americanization process and as a means of upward mobility. New immigrants no longer seek camaraderie through political parties, which they may find too far removed from their traditions. And the children of the old immigrants no longer seek comaraderie through political parties, perhaps because the parties are not homogeneous enough to meet their needs as part of the rising middle class.[8] Then too there is reason to believe that formal education lowers affinity to party, and Americans are clearly becoming more educated.[9] Why should voters cast their ballots for candidates merely because they are Republicans or Democrats when voters now have sufficient analytical ability and information (as well as leisure to join the two) to reach their own conclusions based on whatever factors are important to them?

Without parties, however, elections become more susceptible to appeals of demagogues and passions of the moment. Parties are essential to the governance of a free society. And the quest for responsible parties has been a constant theme of political scientists and reformers of both the right and left. Their search is for a system in which each party puts forth a distinct program, measurably different from the opponents'. They seek parties that nominate candidates who are loyal to the party program and will appeal to the electorate on programmatic grounds, candidates who will, once in office, govern on the basis of the party's ideology.[10] But such a system never can be realized in America.

8. It may be, however, too easy to dismiss the social club function of politics. Examining three state campaigns in 1974, Xandra Kayden found many participants who were there, as one of them put it, "as an escape to meet more people." In an increasingly mobile population in which people tend to remain single longer and there is a high divorce rate, politics—although not necessarily political parties—can still serve as a source of companionship. *Campaign Organization* (Heath, 1978), esp. pp. 59–60.

9. See Jack Dennis, "Support for the Party System by the Mass Public," *American Political Science Review*, vol. 60 (September 1966), pp. 600–15.

10. See Committee on Political Parties of the American Political Science Association, *Toward a More Responsible Two-Party System* (Rinehart, 1950).

The Constitution was written by men who deeply feared factions and designed a form of government that was not a fertile field for the growth of national parties.[11] And even if all the checks and balances, separations of power, and levels of government did not work against strengthening the party system, there is little in the American character or society to encourage the proponents of strong parties.

Voters have proved themselves fiercely nonideological. They are content—if not smug—in their display of independence. "I vote the man, not the party" is more than a cliché: it is a patriotic slogan. Strong attachment to party assumes a willingness to march in lockstep with others, even though a collective position does not conform to individual preferences. This is not something that easily fits the American's self-image. Nor does it readily fit a society of diverse interests. Each person wears too many hats—producer and consumer, religionist and regionalist—to easily accept one set of principles devised by one party.

We are an antiparty people and an antiparty society whose government is organized around a party system. We manage, in part, because there are enough people (a decided minority) who are interested in doing the maintenance work necessary to keep the parties functioning, thus allowing the majority to get on with other chores. Even the party activist, although undoubtedly having a higher quotient of ideology, is motivated in politics by many nonideological considerations, including the joy of participation and the prospect of rewards.

We put up with parties because we cannot think of a better way of organizing our politics. Indeed, there is none. The parties provide some necessary cohesion, which we must have if we are not to choose sides anew every time there is an election, and some historical memory, which is necessary if we are not to start from scratch every time a public official dies, retires, or is defeated.

11. See Federalist Paper no. 10 (first published in *New York Packet*, November 23, 1787); also see President Washington's farewell address of September 17, 1796, warning against the "baneful effects of the spirit of party."

We have no choice. On the basis of what other organizing principle could we wage free elections? A no-party system would create chaos. A system based on special interest groups would be too narrow in scope to handle all the issues that confront us.

From time to time it appears that we are about to splinter into a multiparty system, usually when some prominent figure (Theodore Roosevelt, Robert LaFollette, Henry Wallace, George Wallace, Eugene McCarthy, John Anderson) cannot obtain a dominant place in his own party. But law and tradition are stacked against third parties, and while they may prosper in one election, the system generally reverts quickly to the status quo. There is, of course, a remote possibility that a minor party will become a serious contender for elective offices, as some hoped would happen to Norman Thomas's Socialists in the 1930s. But such groups carry too much doctrinal baggage for most Americans, and their more viable proposals tend to get coopted by the major parties.[12]

Many commentators have made a virtue of the lack of ideology in our parties. As Herbert Agar puts it, "The party is intended to be an organization for 'getting or keeping the patronage of government.' Instead of seeking 'principles,' or 'distinctive tenets,' which can only divide a federal union, the party is intended to seek bargains between the regions, the classes, the other interest groups." This he sees as "a sign of health."[13] There is, of course, a middle ground between parties that stand only for spoils and those that rush to the barricades on every issue. In fact, it fits our history best to locate America's major parties somewhere between these two extremes. And the case that they are intellectually rudderless is often overstated. James L. Sundquist finds that textbooks and other writing on parties are littered with statements such as, "The American majority party is . . . lacking

12. See Daniel A. Mazmanian, *Third Parties in Presidential Elections* (Brookings, 1974).

13. *The Price of Union*, 2d ed. (Houghton Mifflin, 1966), pp. 689–90. Also see E. E. Schattschneider, *Party Government* (Rinehart, 1942).

in party principles."[14] The parties may not be ideological, but their adherents are like-minded. There have to be differences between Democrats and Republicans. Why else would people divide themselves in this way? The Republican party appeals to some, the Democratic party to others, and from time to time the party labels get sorted out. U.S. Senator Don Riegle (Michigan) becomes a Democrat, U.S. Senator Phil Gramm (Texas) becomes a Republican, each finding that he is more like those who call themselves by those names. Moreover, periodically—the Civil War, the New Deal—the whole party alignment comes apart and regroups, clearly because there are enough differences on issues to divide us and unite us. In short, there may not be much ideology in American politics, but there is enough to put us on contending sides. The question should be whether the parties could not better employ these differences—in the form of practical policy recommendations—to the improvement of the country and the party system.

Although the types of material and social rewards that the parties continue to offer are no longer sufficient to ensure their health, there is cause to believe that parties would be strengthened by greater attention to the goals of public policy and problem solving. This is not the same as raising the ideological temperature of politics. Americans are uniquely uninterested in the sorts of pure doctrine that have distinguished many European parties as well as minor parties in this country.

The same forces that have weakened American parties' hold on their constituents—higher levels of education, a rising middle class, more leisure, better means of communications—also work in the direction of promoting purpose in politics. As the parties have declined, there has been a rise in public interest lobbying groups—Common Cause, Ralph Nader's organizations, the Sierra Club and other environmental units, and a variety of single-cause groups working in such areas as prison reform, consumer

14. *Dynamics of the Party System*, rev. ed. (Brookings, 1983), pp. 324–25.

protection, pro- and antiabortion, and promotion of the welfare of specific minorities. Such entities sop up the energies of activists that formerly went into maintaining the party system and, although some would vigorously deny it, they usually develop a strong antiparty bias that further works to undermine the parties' viability. [15]

People are concerned about the effects of government action on their lives and the failure of government to find solutions to pressing problems, yet the parties continue to see themselves primarily in terms of mobilizing the vote, a purely organizational function, and performing such other supportive duties as providing entry to government, raising money, and undertaking certain social activities. Thus they are still playing by the old rules, which are increasingly irrelevant to larger numbers of citizens. This is part of the explanation for high levels of distrust in politics, low turnout of voters, decreased party registration, and the apathy of the young about party involvement.

Increasing their acceptability among the voters by making the parties more responsive, however, will not necessarily strengthen the two-party system. If the system is to become more viable, the separation between candidates and officeholders and their parties must be decreased; in other words, incentives or punishments must be designed to make candidates more beholden to their parties for winning office and more dependent on them once in office.

According to the basic rules of political organizations, the two ways to reach this goal should be to centralize and to discipline. But for most of our history, American parties have been unwilling to do either. "The political party, at least in the United States," writes James Q. Wilson, "is a conspicuous exception to the general tendency for society to become increasingly organized, rationalized, and bureaucratized."[16] Frank J. Sorauf reasons that the semiautonomous condition of state and local party organizations in America has become "well enough established to resist

15. See Andrew S. McFarland, *Common Cause* (Chatham House, 1984).
16. *Political Organizations* (Basic Books, 1973), p. 95.

even those centralizing tendencies."[17] As government has become more centralized, the decentralized party system has become even less capable of coping with public problems.

Particularly in legislative settings, the parties have rarely disciplined mavericks. Perhaps this is a part of our strong sense of pragmatism. Is it better to have a sometime party member (such as a legislator who may not toe the line on many issues, but at least votes "right" on who should control the legislative machinery) or no party member at all? For example, Senator Harry Byrd, Jr., of Virginia deserted the Democrats to run as an independent in 1970 and 1976, yet was allowed to continue to sit on the Democratic side of the aisle. The inability to maintain legislative discipline also stems from regional needs. Southern legislators, Western legislators, farm state legislators may have more in common with other legislators from their locales, regardless of party affiliation, than they do with members of their own party from other regions. Then, too, party discipline is weakened by Americans' acceptance of the Burkean theory of representation in which legislators are expected to vote their consciences.

There has, however, been a surprising willingness in both parties (particularly the Democratic party) to assume greater control over their own reproductive systems, the bodies that choose the persons who will be their presidential nominees. This trend began fairly modestly in 1956 when the Democratic convention voted a loyalty oath, requiring state parties to "undertake to assure" that the Democratic presidential nominee would appear on the ballot. In 1964 the Democrats adopted a national no-discrimination rule, forcing state parties to select convention delegates "regardless of race, color, creed or national origin." As a result, the 1968 convention refused to seat the regular Mississippi delegation.[18] Changes adopted in 1972 and

17. *Party Politics in America* (Little, Brown, 1968), p. 405.
18. See Austin Ranney, "The Democratic Party's Delegate Selection Reforms, 1968–76," in Allan P. Sindler, ed., *America in the Seventies* (Little, Brown, 1977), p. 164.

1976 imposed national rules on the selection of state delegates and made the rules stick, notably by expelling from the 1972 convention the delegates that had been sent there by Chicago's powerful mayor, Richard Daley. This development was remarkable in a country that is often referred to as having no national parties but only a collection of fifty state parties.[19] Presumably, it should have had measurable effect in strengthening the two-party system.

But it did not. The reverse happened. The new national Democratic rules caused a proliferation of state primaries, producing a type of delegate who was even more wedded to candidate and divorced from party.[20] At the 1976 convention only 18 percent of the party's U.S. senators were delegates or alternates, down from 68 percent in 1968; governors declined from 83 percent to 47 percent; House members dropped from 39 percent to 15 percent. Shocked by the consequences of reform, traditionalists, led by North Carolina Governor James Hunt, convinced the party to create a new category of superdelegate, consisting of party functionaries and public officials. The group accounted for slightly more than 14 percent of the vote at the 1984 convention. In 1988 the superdelegates will include all members of the Democratic National Committee, 80 percent of the party's members of Congress, and all Democratic governors.[21] The change is a partial response to political scientists' and political journalists' call for peer review, meaning that those who best

19. Most recently, the Democratic National Committee threatened penalties against the Minnesota and South Dakota parties for scheduling their delegate selection earlier in 1988 than party rules allow. The state organizations agreed to modest changes. See Maralee Schwartz, "Democrats Rescind Penalties Against 2 State Delegations," *Washington Post*, October 8, 1987.

20. The history of the Democratic party's reforms is well told in Austin Ranney, *Curing the Mischiefs of Faction* (University of California Press, 1975); and Byron E. Shafer, *Quiet Revolution: The Struggle for the Democratic Party and the Shaping of Post-Reform Politics* (Russell Sage Foundation, 1983). For the most up-to-date assessment, see Austin Ranney, "Farewell to Reform—Almost," *Society*, vol. 24 (May–June 1987), pp. 29–38.

21. Rhodes Cook, "Democratic Party Sets Count for Largest-Ever Convention," *CQ* (November 29, 1986), p. 2987.

know the presidential contenders should have a greater voice in selection.[22]

For reasons that have been considered good and sufficient by a great many Americans, the United States is not going to govern itself under a strong and disciplined party system. No scholars' agenda will make it otherwise. Still, the parties need not be hapless giants. America may have moved permanently to candidate-centered campaigns, but the parties have some control over the candidates. No candidate can expect to be president without a major party line on the voting machines, and this is the parties' to give or withhold. The honor of running for president should be based on past conduct and future expectations. As such, the parties should decree that their nominations will be given to persons who abide by certain rules of conduct— enforceable by the parties—during the preconvention period and will then conduct their postconvention campaigns along prescribed ethical lines. In short, when we choose between a Republican and a Democrat the parties have an obligation to protect their brand names, and their consumers.

22. Yet Thomas E. Mann concludes that the impact of the superdelegates in 1984 was modest. See his "Elected Officials and the Politics of Presidential Selection," in Austin Ranney, ed., *The American Elections of 1984* (Duke University Press, 1985), pp. 100–28.

NINE

"Why Great Men Are Not Chosen
Presidents"

ON OCTOBER 22, 1888, as voters were getting
ready to decide whether Grover Cleveland should continue to
reside in the White House or should be evicted in favor of
Benjamin Harrison, the future Lord Bryce (he was made a
viscount in 1913) signed off on what was to be the first edition
of *The American Commonwealth*. This massive description of
late nineteenth century democracy in the United States would
have a profound influence on a generation of political scientists,
but today it is recalled largely because of the name of its eighth
chapter: "Why Great Men Are Not Chosen Presidents."

Although James Bryce was Regius Professor of Civil Law at
Oxford when he wrote *The American Commonwealth*, his approach was journalistic, a reporting of data gathered largely by
talking to politicians and others. As a conventional British
gentleman, albeit one who loved America, he might have been
offended by this classification: journalists were not gentlemen.
But in a sense Bryce was the Theodore H. White of his day, and
the impact of his book was not unlike that of the first *Making of
the President* when it was published in 1961.

Bryce was fascinated by the presidential selection process,
which he considered largely controlled by party organizations
that determined nominations and preferred mediocre candidates.

While he had high praise for presidents "down till the election
of Andrew Jackson," he considered subsequent executives, with

several exceptions, to be "personally insignificant."[1] It was apparently the most recent presidencies that loomed largest in his vision. (Even Oxford dons cannot repeal the laws of perspective.) When he first visited the United States in 1870, the White House was occupied by Ulysses S. Grant; the presidents on his next visits were Rutherford B. Hayes (1880) and Chester A. Arthur (1883). His low opinion of American chief executives, Bryce might have claimed, was based on personal observation.[2] Yet to have made his case for the debasing influence of parties, he would have had to prove that the parties pushed aside more distinguished figures. And this was not necessarily what happened. Should the Republicans have preferred John Sherman to Hayes? Should the Democrats have chosen Thomas Bayard over Cleveland? There are times that seem to lack great men. Perhaps Bryce was merely observing one of history's troughs, regardless of how the candidates were chosen.

Bryce never felt the need to define greatness. He apparently thought that any intelligent person would recognize its presence or absence. This tends to turn the hunt for great men into something of a parlor game. Why, for instance, did he not pay more attention to early twentieth century nominees? (The book was extensively revised in 1910 and 1914, with editions coming out until 1922, the year of his death.) During this period the Republicans and Democrats nominated what a British gentleman should have concluded were some of the finest candidates since the nation's founding generation. For sheer brilliance it would be hard to surpass Theodore Roosevelt, William Howard Taft, Woodrow Wilson, and Charles Evans Hughes. And while the

---

1. James Bryce, *The American Commonwealth* (Macmillan, 1888), vol. 1, p. 80. All references are to this edition unless otherwise noted. For biographical information on Bryce, see Robert G. McCloskey's entry in *International Encyclopedia of the Social Sciences*; and H. A. L. Fisher, *James Bryce* (Macmillan, 1927), esp. vol. 1, pp. 222–42.

2. Similarly, James MacGregor Burns, apparently still entranced in the mid-1960s by a system that had selected John F. Kennedy, challenged Bryce. See "Why Great Men Are Chosen President," in his *Presidential Government* (Houghton Mifflin, 1966), pp. 295–303.

populist William Jennings Bryan would not have appealed to Lord Bryce, the Great Commoner was a person of extraordinary qualities as well. All but one of Bryce's revised editions contain a footnote stating that "of Presidents since 1900 it is not yet time to speak"; still, he did change the 1910 text to read, "Great men have not *often* been chosen Presidents."[3] (By leaving himself wiggle room to elevate his friend Roosevelt to the pantheon of greatness, Bryce also aided the cause of Anglo-American friendship, for which he had assumed some responsibility upon appointment as British ambassador to Washington in 1907.)

Necessarily, Bryce recognized that some great men would prove to be not-great presidents (Grant), and that others of more modest prepresidential achievement (Lincoln) would become great presidents. There are bound to be surprises galore once a person enters the White House.

The title of Bryce's essay still reflects historical fact in that no major party has nominated a woman for president, which suggests the obvious: whenever an excluded group is allowed into the pool of presidential contenders there will be more possibilities, some of whom might be great. When a religious barrier came down with the 1928 nomination of Alfred E. Smith, a Roman Catholic, and with John F. Kennedy's election in 1960, the pool expanded, but not the type of contenders. Smith and Kennedy were professional politicians, differing from the other contenders in their generation primarily in religious affiliation. The first woman presidential nominee most likely will have been vice president, as the first woman vice presidential nominee of a major party was a member of Congress.

If Bryce's evaluation of the American system is tinged by a parliamentarian's preference for the way prime ministers are selected, however, his critique cannot be dismissed as mere chauvinism.[4] He argued that in the America he had observed,

3. Bryce (1910 edition), vol. 1, p. 83. Italics added.
4. For a more balanced and rigorous comparative examination of the two systems, see Hugh Heclo, "Presidential and Prime Ministerial Selection," in

great men were less drawn to politics than to "the business of developing the material resources of the country"; that compared with European countries, American political life offered "fewer opportunities for personal distinction"; that "eminent men make more enemies"; and that the American voter did "not object to mediocrity." But the heart of his argument was that great men were not chosen president because of the party system. Political bosses, he observed, gauged the strength of local organizations and the loyalty of voters and then calculated which candidate would add the right demographics to ensure victory. The objective was winning, not governing. He illustrated:

> On a railway journey in the Far West in 1883 I fell in with two newspaper men from the State of Indiana, who were taking their holiday. The conversation turned on the next presidential election. They spoke hopefully of the chances for nomination by their party of an Indiana man, a comparatively obscure person, whose name I had never heard. I expressed some surprise that he should be thought of. They observed that he had done well in State politics, that there was nothing against him, that Indiana would work for him. "But," I rejoined, "ought you not to have a man of more commanding character. There is Senator A. Everybody tells me that he is the shrewdest and most experienced man in your party, and that he has a perfectly clean record. Why not run him?" "Why, yes," they answered, "that is all true. But you see he comes from a small State, and we have got that State already. Besides, he wasn't in the war. Our man was. Indiana's vote is worth having, and if our man is run, we can carry Indiana."[5]

The paradox of revisiting Lord Bryce one hundred years after he said great men were not chosen presidents because of political parties is that political parties are in decline, as we have noted, and there is still no certainty that great men will be chosen president.

"The media in the United States are the new political parties," James David Barber contends. "The old political parties are

Donald R. Matthews, ed., *Perspectives on Presidential Selection* (Brookings, 1973), pp. 19–48.
5. Bryce, vol. 1, pp. 74–75, 78.

gone."[6] Former Democratic House Speaker Thomas P. O'Neill has said that members who entered Congress since the upheavals of Watergate and the Vietnam War "had no loyalty to the party whatsoever. They looked down on it. They said, 'The party didn't elect me, and I'm not beholden to the party.'"[7] Campaign consultant David Garth even notes that "the [political] boss is a plus to have against you."[8]

Although some experts see new life in the old parties,[9] the way presidential candidates get nominated has irrevocably changed since Bryce's day. In 1901 Florida enacted the first presidential primary law, an invention designed to take nominations out of the hands of the party regulars. By 1980, primaries selected 71 percent of the delegates to the Democratic national convention. The number of primaries dropped in 1984, but by then the news media had turned important party caucuses, such as Iowa's, into quasi primaries. Accompanied by much greater voter independence and major technological changes, notably the coming of television, the new system was expected to produce a different type of presidential nominee. As one careful student of presidential politics wrote in 1981, "Neither Jimmy Carter nor Ronald Reagan were unlikely nominees for the system under which we now choose our presidents, as Harry Truman and Thomas E. Dewey were not unlikely nominees for the system under which we once chose them."[10]

6. Quoted by Gary R. Orren, "Thinking about the Press and Government," in Martin Linsky, ed., *Impact: How the Press Affects Federal Policymaking* (Norton, 1986), p. 10.

7. Quoted in Steven V. Roberts, "For New Speaker, New Role Is Seen," *New York Times*, December 8, 1986.

8. Quoted in Alan Eysen, "Tracking the Decline of Party Organizations," *Newsday*, April 23, 1981.

9. See David E. Price, *Bringing Back the Parties* (CQ Press, 1984); Xandra Kayden and Eddie Mahe, Jr., *The Party Goes On* (Basic Books, 1985); and A. James Reichley, "The Rise of National Parties," in John E. Chubb and Paul E. Peterson, eds., *The New Direction in American Politics* (Brookings, 1985), pp. 175–200; for a less optimistic view, see Martin F. Wattenberg, *The Decline of American Political Parties 1952–1980* (Harvard University Press, 1984).

10. Byron E. Shafer, "Anti-Party Politics," *Public Interest*, no. 63 (Spring 1981), pp. 95–96.

A tenet of political science and political journalism is that as the process changes so too do the outcomes. This notion is laudable and essentially optimistic. We are capable of changing the way we nominate presidential candidates, ergo we can improve the quality of presidents. Then if improvement schemes turn out otherwise, we can rail against the shortsightedness of reformers or the ignorance of those who fail to foresee unanticipated consequences—or both. Obviously the rules have affected some contenders' prospects in the past. Neither James K. Polk nor Woodrow Wilson would have been nominated had not Democratic conventions operated under a two-thirds rule, which was repealed in 1936.[11] Jimmy Carter's treasurer claims that his candidate could not have won the 1976 nomination had not the law been changed to limit the amount that "fat cats" could give to campaigns.[12] The rules will continue to affect contenders' prospects unevenly. Indeed, there are those who suggest that candidates who best figure out how to use the rules to their own advantage deserve to win, although others argue that the skills needed to win a nomination are not presidential skills.[13]

But do changes in process really result in different kinds of persons seeking the presidency? Following the 1968 and 1972 Democratic conventions, party commissions imposed major changes on the demographic mix and selection of delegates. To abide by the new rules, many states established primary elections. Moving from a caucus to a primary system meant that the media would play a much more important role in candidates' strategies. Changes in finance rules also changed candidates' strategies.[14] But analyses

11. At the Democratic convention of 1844 Martin Van Buren received 55 percent of the vote on the first ballot; on the tenth ballot at the 1912 Democratic convention, Champ Clark had 51 percent of the vote. See Richard C. Bain and Judith H. Parris, *Convention Decisions and Voting Records*, 2d ed. (Brookings, 1973), app. C.

12. See Warren Weaver, Jr., "Aide Says New Limits on Contributions Helped Carter Campaign," *New York Times*, July 20, 1976.

13. See Nelson W. Polsby, *Consequences of Party Reform* (Oxford University Press, 1983).

14. See Gary R. Orren and Nelson W. Polsby, eds., *Media and Momentum* (Chatham House, 1987), pp. 1–4.

suggesting that the nominees chosen under the new rules were different in kind because of these changes may simply be placing too much emphasis on too few cases. After all, there have been only eight nominations since 1972, and four of them were already sitting presidents. For every obscure senator from a small state who has been nominated in recent times (George McGovern of South Dakota), one can find an earlier obscure senator from a small state (Franklin Pierce of New Hampshire, for example). An obscure governor (Jimmy Carter of Georgia) can be juxtaposed against an earlier obscure governor (Alfred M. Landon of Kansas). History is wondrously full of contrary examples to confound theories.

One consequence of the new system, some say, is that successful candidates are more extreme in their views, in part because activists on specific issues are overrepresented among primary voters. Observing the 1952 Democratic presidential convention, Richard Rovere compared contenders' activities with a game of musical chairs in which each chair represents an ideological position (liberal through conservative); if a chair is occupied when the music stops, the player is forced to seek a different chair. (Averell Harriman unexpectedly found himself in the liberal seat, Alben W. Barkley was suddenly thrust into the conservative seat.)[15] In terms of Rovere's formulation, when Hubert Humphrey, a lifelong liberal, entered the race in 1968, he discovered Robert Kennedy already sitting in the liberal chair and had to find another place to sit. This does not mean that Humphrey or Kennedy (or Walter Mondale or Gary Hart, George Bush or Robert Dole) as president would respond to similar pressures in dissimilar ways. Quite the contrary: professional politicians are likely to have similar responses. They are not clones, of course, but they tend to weigh opportunities and

15. See Richard Rovere, "Letter from Chicago," *New Yorker* (August 2, 1952), pp. 58–59. Perhaps the best example of musical chairs in recent years is John Anderson's move to the left in the 1980 Republican nomination contest. See Gerald Pomper and others, *The Election of 1980* (Chatham House, 1981), pp. 13–14.

constraints on the same scale. Hence some of the claims that today's candidates are markedly more ideological than those in the past may be simply taking too literally the images that contestants have drawn of themselves (and of their opponents) during recent intraparty disputes. The new system's winners to date have been Reagan and Carter, one of the most ideological candidates and one of the least.[16] The jury is still out on this question.

Following his defeat in 1984, Walter Mondale publicly worried that because of the voters' growing reliance on television, future presidential candidates would have to be masters of the "twenty-second snip, the angle, the shtick, whatever it is. . . ."[17] Having just been run over by a former actor, who also happened to be one of the great politicians of this century, Mondale commands sympathy. One could imagine Alf Landon making the same statement in 1936 after his landslide loss to Franklin D. Roosevelt, although Landon's concern would have been directed against the impact of radio. Politicians will adapt the technology at hand to their needs. What is most surprising about the TV age is that besides Reagan and John Kennedy, the others who have won presidential nominations—Nixon, Johnson, Goldwater, Humphrey, McGovern, Carter, Ford, and Mondale—are no more telegenic than any cross section of middle-aged white males. Nor do the politicians who are at the starting gate for 1988 appear to have come from Central Casting. All of which suggests how little things change as the nation moves from party democracy to media democracy.

Throughout American history those picked to be major party presidential candidates, above all else, have been professional politicians. This is even more true today than it was in the nineteenth century. The reason is that "just wars" generate viable amateur candidates. Between 1824, when Andrew Jackson first

16. See Carl M. Brauer, *Presidential Transitions* (Oxford University Press, 1986), p. 258.
17. Quoted in Elizabeth Drew, "A Political Journal," *New Yorker* (December 3, 1984), p. 174.

ran for president, and 1892, when Benjamin Harrison last ran, persons who had been generals were nominated in all but three elections (1844, 1860, 1884). In this century just the Second World War yielded a nominee, Dwight Eisenhower.[18] The twenty-nine men nominated by the major parties since 1900 have a collective record of officeholding that includes service as governors (thirteen), senators (nine), members of the House of Representatives (nine), vice presidents (eight), judges (three), and cabinet members (two).[19] These men have moved through a maze of political jobs in order to reach the ultimate goal, and in eighty-four years only two members of that charmed circle—business executive Wendell L. Willkie and General Eisenhower—had never held civil public office before running for president.[20]

To draw career histories of presidential nominees, thus illustrating the extent to which they have come from the ranks of professional politicians, is not to imply that the only way to reach the White House is to climb a political ladder, step by step, starting perhaps in the state legislature and gradually rising to a governorship or a seat in the Senate before attempting the final ascent. While the ladder metaphor reflects the most common

18. To date the only military men who have successfully used the Vietnam War as a political springboard in statewide elections have been two antiwar leaders (Robert Kerrey and John Kerry, both of whom served in Vietnam) and two former prisoners of war (Jeremiah Denton and John McCain). The war's top general, William Westmoreland, was defeated in his attempt to become a governor.

19. The Governors were William McKinley, Theodore Roosevelt, Woodrow Wilson, Charles Evans Hughes, James Cox, Calvin Coolidge, Alfred E. Smith, Franklin D. Roosevelt, Alfred M. Landon, Thomas E. Dewey, Adlai E. Stevenson, Jimmy Carter, and Ronald Reagan. The senators were Warren G. Harding, Harry S. Truman, John F. Kennedy, Richard M. Nixon, Lyndon B. Johnson, Barry Goldwater, Hubert H. Humphrey, George McGovern, and Walter Mondale. Members of the House of Representatives were William Jennings Bryan, McKinley, Cox, John W. Davis, Nixon, Kennedy, Johnson, McGovern, and Gerald R. Ford. Theodore Roosevelt, Coolidge, Truman, Nixon, Johnson, Humphrey, Ford, and Mondale were vice presidents; Alton B. Parker, William Howard Taft, and Hughes were judges; and Taft and Herbert Hoover were cabinet members.

20. See Donald R. Matthews, "Presidential Nominations: Process and Outcomes," in James David Barber, ed., *Choosing the President* (Prentice-Hall, 1974), esp. pp. 45–46.

pattern, lateral entry into a governor's chair or Congress is not uncommon. Ronald Reagan was not the first person to transfer fame or wealth earned outside politics into success as an office-seeker.

With the decline of parties, it would be expected that more persons could reach elected office without serving an apprentice-ship—and this has happened.[21] It should be remembered, how-ever, that Americans always have had what Robert Dahl calls "our belief in the supposed superiority of the amateur," a belief, he contends, that "we hold to only in politics and in the athletic activities of a small number of private colleges and universities whose alumni permit them the luxury of bad football teams."[22] Twentieth century Americans may attribute special leadership qualities to astronauts, but nineteenth century Americans attrib-uted similar qualities to explorers. Recall that John C. Frémont, the Pathfinder of the Rockies, was the first Republican presidential nominee in 1856. A journalist-celebrity, Horace Greeley, was the Democratic choice for president in 1872. Those advantaged by birth, whether an Adams, a Harrison, or a Roosevelt, have had a leg up since colonial times.[23] Nor did the cleric-turned-politician begin with Pat Robertson and Jesse Jackson. The Muhlenberg family of Pennsylvania, for example, sent three ordained ministers to Congress. In contrast, the businessman-celebrity has fared poorly in politics, despite Calvin Coolidge's axiom that the business of America is business.[24]

21. See Dennis M. Simon and David T. Canon, "Actors, Athletes, and Astronauts: Amateurism and Changing Career Paths in the United States Senate," paper delivered at the 1984 annual meeting of the Midwest Political Science Association.

22. "Foreword" in Joseph A. Schlesinger, How They Became Governor (Michigan State University, 1957).

23. There have been some 700 families in which 2 or more members have served in the U.S. Congress. See Stephen Hess, America's Political Dynasties (Doubleday, 1966), p. 1.

24. George Romney went from being chief executive of American Motors to being governor of Michigan and Charles Percy went from the presidency of Bell and Howell to the U.S. Senate, but the White House was an illusive goal for them and such other magnates as Henry Ford and William Randolph Hearst.

With the passage of time, what changes is which groups of celebrities turn to politics. The sports celebrity, such as Jack Kemp, is a recent political phenomenon. At least the only nineteenth century athlete-politico that comes to mind, also an upstate New York congressman, was John Morrissey, who had been world heavyweight boxing champion.

Contenders for presidential nominations may have to appeal to different selectors as the selection process changes, but the winners in the TV-and-primaries era are not unprecedented in what they offer the voters. Whether today's nominees get there by climbing a political ladder or by lateral entry, they still would be recognizable to Lord Bryce. The system in Bryce's time promoted those experienced in coalition building; today's system promotes expert persuaders. Both are qualities considered presidentially important. The finite differences between politicians running for president under the old system and politicians chosen by newer rules are mainly of interest to those who make a living sniffing such fine distinctions.

The idea of a political career ladder based on ambition was masterfully presented by Joseph A. Schlesinger. "Ambition lies at the heart of politics," he wrote in 1966. "Politics thrive on the hope of preferment and the drive for office."[25] Others then used Schlesinger's theory to show how elimination occurs as politicians attempt to move up the rungs.[26] The final ambition, of course,

25. *Ambition and Politics: Political Careers in the United States* (Rand McNally, 1966), p. 1.
26. See Kenneth Prewitt and William Nowlin, "Political Ambitions and the Behavior of Incumbent Politicians," *Western Political Quarterly*, vol. 22 (June 1969), pp. 248–308; Michael L. Mezey, "Ambition Theory and the Office of Congressman," *Journal of Politics*, vol. 32 (August 1970), pp. 503–79; Jeff Fishel, "Ambition and the Political Vocation: Congressional Challengers in American Politics," *Journal of Politics*, vol. 33 (February 1971), pp. 25–56; Gordon S. Black, "A Theory of Political Ambition: Career Choices and the Role of Structural Incentives," *American Political Science Review*, vol. 66 (March 1972), pp. 144–59; Paul L. Hain, "Age, Ambitions, and Political Careers: The Middle-Age Crisis," *Western Political Quarterly*, vol. 27 (June 1974), pp. 265–74; David W. Rohde, "Risk-Bearing and Progressive Ambition: The Case of Members of the United States House of Representatives," *American Journal of Political Science*,

is the presidency, which rises so high above the other steps as to constitute a separate ladder. The dramatic distance between the presidency and lower levels of public employment has consequences for what Schlesinger calls progressive ambition ("The politician aspires to attain an office more important than the one he now seeks or is holding").[27] While no person becomes vice president without being willing to become president, what of the others whose jobs make them eligible to be mentioned as prospective presidential candidates? Ordinary ambition can carry a supplicant to the level of U.S. senator or governor, but then, because of the wide gap that must be bridged, another dynamic takes over. President Eisenhower once mused that the only thing successful politicians have in common is that they all married above themselves. But the only common denominator I have observed for those politicians who would be president is the depth of their ambition. What distinguishes the candidates seeking their parties' 1988 presidential nominations from other high office-holders of their generation?[28] Not their intelligence, accomplishments, style, or the reality of their prospects. What distinguishes them is *presidential ambition*, the ultimate in progressive ambition.

In applying the concept of progressive ambition to the presidency, scholars assume almost all U.S. senators would accept the highest office if it were offered to them without cost or risk. It cannot be. Costs of running for president can be very great. In some cases the candidate must give up a Senate seat, as Barry Goldwater did in 1964. In all cases there are physical costs.

---

vol. 23 (February 1979), pp. 1–26; Paul Brace, "Progressive Ambition in the House: A Probabilistic Approach," *Journal of Politics*, vol. 46 (May 1984), pp. 556–71; and Paul R. Abramson, John H. Aldrich, and David W. Rohde, "Progressive Ambition among United States Senators: 1972–1988," *Journal of Politics*, vol. 49 (February 1987), pp. 3–35.

27. Schlesinger, *Ambition and Politics*, p. 10.

28. At the time of this writing, the Democratic contenders are Bruce Babbitt, Michael Dukakis, Richard Gephardt, Albert Gore, Jr., Jesse Jackson, and Paul Simon; the Republicans are George Bush, Robert Dole, Pierre du Pont, Alexander Haig, Jack Kemp, and Pat Robertson.

When Senator Dale Bumpers declined to become a candidate for the 1988 Democratic nomination, he publicly questioned whether he had the stamina for the "18 months of 18-hour days" that presidential campaigns can require.[29] There are financial costs. Donald Rumsfeld and Paul Laxalt said they were not prepared to go deeply into debt in order to seek the 1988 Republican nomination. Potential candidates must also consider the almost total loss of privacy. What are the effects that running for president can have on a candidate's family? Whether to expose spouse, children, even parents and siblings to this ordeal could be considered the test of what divides those with presidential ambition from others who are simply eligible to be contenders. Meg Greenfield wrote, "People who have made a serious run for the office or been around those that do will tell you that until you have experienced a presidential candidacy close up, nothing prepares you for the total onslaught on your life and that of your family that comes with the campaign."[30] Mario Cuomo seemed to have all the political attributes necessary to run for president in 1988. He was reelected governor of New York in 1986 by the biggest gubernatorial landslide in his state's history and had more than $3 million left over from that campaign. But he was not prepared to subject his family to "the total onslaught" and announced that he would not seek the Democratic nomination.[31]

In their imaginative attempt to factor risk-taking potential into the equation, Paul R. Abramson, John H. Aldrich, and David W. Rohde show that Democratic senators who are proven risk takers have been "a good deal more likely to run for president

29. See Paul Taylor, "Bumpers Decides Against Presidential Bid," *Washington Post*, March 21, 1987.

30. "The Bradley-Nunn Problem," *Washington Post*, November 11, 1986.

31. Commenting on his 1986 campaign, Cuomo said, "What it makes you think about is look, is this really an ego exercise by you? Look at what it's done to your kids. What about [daughter] Madeline? Three times she's stopped for a red light. Then she's in the newspapers. Somebody refers to her as a bleached blonde. I mean, I could strangle the guy." Quoted in Paul Taylor, "Cuomo Sends the Word That He's Weighing Entering the Fray," *Washington Post*, January 25, 1987; also see Michael Oreskes, "Cuomo Leaves the Ring," *Washington Journalism Review* (April 1987), p. 17.

[since 1972] than those who were not."[32] Yet as their analysis of the 1984 election shows, seventeen Democratic senators were "well situated" to run for president and thirteen of them chose not to make the race.[33]

This finding is in keeping with my survey of Senate news coverage: ten senators received 50 percent and thirty-five senators received 5 percent of the national media attention in 1983.[34] Some of the underexposed senators were too old or too young to be of interest to the national press corps. Their time had passed or will come. But most of the senators who are rarely, if ever, on network TV do not wish to be president. Quentin Burdick, one of seventeen senators never seen on the networks' 1,095 evening news programs during 1983, told a Washington reporter, "I'm very conscious about what they're saying in North Dakota, but not outside the state. I'm not running for president." His press secretary added, "To him if it doesn't happen in North Dakota, it doesn't happen."[35] In any event, Burdick's age, eighty in 1988, barred him from a run for the presidency. Yet many younger senators will never offer themselves as candidates for the top office. The Senate is their ceiling of progressive ambition. Some of them may have judged that they are not qualified. But mainly their reasons are deeply personal, beyond scholars' tools of measurement. Strangely, perhaps, a Senate leadership position (given the ego and attributes that it implies) fails to correlate with presidential ambition, which strikes some leaders (Lyndon Johnson, Robert Dole) and not others (Mike Mansfield, Hugh Scott).

How best to describe presidential ambition (apparently so much more intense than senatorial ambition)? William Howard

32. "Progressive Ambition," p. 13.
33. *Change and Continuity in the 1984 Elections* (CQ Press, 1986), p. 16. The percentage of Republican senators who would not have run for president if Reagan had retired would have been even higher.
34. *The Ultimate Insiders: U.S. Senators in the National Media* (Brookings, 1986), pp. 11, 16.
35. Bill Blocher, "Study of U.S. Senators Is Worthless," *Williston* (N. Dak.) *Herald*, May 13, 1986; and Steve Adams, "Study Calls Burdick 'Under-achiever,'" *Minot* (N. Dak.) *Daily News*, May 10, 1986.

Taft may have come close in a story he told about a friend's "little daughter Mary":

> As he came walking home after a business day, she ran out from the house to greet him, all aglow with the importance of what she wished to tell him. She said, "Papa, I am the best scholar in the class." The father's heart throbbed with pleasure as he inquired, "Why, Mary, you surprise me. When did the teacher tell you? This afternoon?" "Oh, no," Mary's reply was, "the teacher didn't tell me—I just noticed it myself."[36]

Taft's gentle tale was his way of chiding Teddy Roosevelt for placing him in a presidential class with James Buchanan, while placing himself in a class with Lincoln. But it was TR's concept of the presidency as a stewardship that separates the modern era from the nineteenth century. "My view," he wrote, "was that every executive officer [read president] . . . was a steward of the people bound actively and affirmatively to do all he could for the people, and not to content himself with the negative merit of keeping his talents undamaged in a napkin."[37] Indeed, given the Rooseveltian way of doing the president's business, Bryce's 1910 edition deleted a paragraph designed to remind Britons that the U.S. president "ought not to address meetings, except on ornamental and (usually) non-political occasions, that he cannot submit bills nor otherwise influence the action of the legislature."[38]

It may well be, of course, that in the days when presidents "ought not to address meetings," presidential ambition was less the motor force that governed the number and kind of contenders. After all, William Howard Taft did not have presidential ambition in 1908 (TR had it for him). Deeply deadlocked nineteenth century conventions sometimes produced surprised winners, notably Horatio Seymour, the Democrats' choice in 1868, who was so opposed to becoming the nominee that the convention

36. William Howard Taft, *Our Chief Magistrate and His Powers* (Columbia University Press, 1925), p. 144.

37. *The Autobiography of Theodore Roosevelt*, Wayne Andrews, ed. (Octagon, 1975), p. 197.

38. Bryce, vol. 1, p. 76.

quickly adjourned before he could refuse the honor.[39] Today, however, before submitting oneself to the obligations of being "the leader of the free world," one might apply the litmus test of ambition stated by John F. Kennedy, who told 1960 audiences:

> I want to be a President who acts as well as reacts—who originates programs as well as study groups—who masters complex problems as well as one-page memorandums. I want to be a President who is Chief Executive in every sense of the word—who responds to a problem, not by hoping his subordinates will act, but by directing them to act—a President who is willing to take the responsibility for getting things done, and take the blame if they are not done right.[40]

One recognizes the hyperbole of the moment. Still, something more distinguishes Kennedy's statement from the garden-variety ambition of most politicians (perhaps *chutzpa*, the Yiddish word that Leo Rosten translates as "presumption-plus-arrogance such as no other word, and no other language, can do justice to").[41] Or as Alexander Haig urged the voters of New Hampshire on the day in 1987 that he announced his candidacy, "Inside this exterior, militant, turf-conscious, excessively ambitious demeanor

39. See Malcolm Moos and Stephen Hess, *Hats in the Ring: The Making of Presidential Candidates* (Random House, 1960), p. 28. It is true, of course, that the old system produced more deadlocked conventions, but dark horse nominees were a decidedly mixed bag in terms of quality and should not be romanticized by those who miss not having an opportunity to watch a convention of politicians trying to dig itself out of a hole. A checklist of dark horse nominees (who were behind on the first ballot and won after more than four ballots): James K. Polk (1844), Franklin Pierce (1852), Winfield Scott (1852), Horatio Seymour (1868), Rutherford B. Hayes (1876), James A. Garfield (1880), Benjamin Harrison (1888), William Jennings Bryan (1896), Woodrow Wilson (1912), James Cox (1920), Warren G. Harding (1920), John W. Davis (1924), and Wendell Willkie (1940).

40. Quoted in James MacGregor Burns, *Leadership* (Harper and Row, 1978), p. 394.

41. *The Joys of Yiddish* (Pocket Books, 1970), p. 93. Overriding ambition is not limited to politicians, of course; it was even stressed as a characteristic of the great theologian Reinhold Niebuhr in a sympathetic essay by Wilson Carey McWilliams, "A Glorious Discontent," *Freedom at Issue*, no. 92–93 (November–December 1986), p. 21.

is a heart as big as all outdoors."[42] If this looks like a strictly contemporary phenomenon, however, consider William Jennings Bryan, thirty-six years old in 1896, a former two-term member of the House of Representatives from Nebraska, most recently defeated for the U.S. Senate, who won the Democratic presidential nomination. Or Thomas E. Dewey, thirty-eight, New York City district attorney, defeated Republican candidate for governor of New York, who almost captured his party's presidential nomination in 1940. Yes, the serious candidates are a self-anointed breed whose ambition sets the contours of presidential selection.

Note that not all presidential contenders really expect to get the nod. Some are in the race primarily to further policy goals or to focus attention on the needs of certain groups or to advance themselves in other pursuits. Archconservative Patrick Buchanan, for example, thought about running for the 1988 Republican nomination because "there is no better forum to advance the ideas you believe in and to give them elevation. . . ."[43] It is only the serious candidate to whom must be attributed the italicized form of presidential ambition.

William Herndon said of his law partner, Abraham Lincoln, "His ambition was a little engine that knew no rest," and Alexander and Juliette George wrote of the "insatiable" and "compulsive" ambition that governed Woodrow Wilson's career.[44] Yet psychological insights cannot predict when an ambition will turn presidential. Franklin Roosevelt was said to view the presidency as "his birthright."[45] But Jimmy Carter claims that he did not see himself as belonging in the White House until 1971 and 1972, when he met "other presidential hopefuls, and I lost my

42. Quoted in David Shribman, "Haig Embarks on 1988 Quest for Presidency," *Wall Street Journal*, March 25, 1987.

43. Quoted in John B. Judis, "White House Vigilante," *New Republic* (January 26, 1987), p. 17.

44. William H. Herndon and Jesse W. Weik, *Herndon's Life of Lincoln: The History of Personal Recollections of Abraham Lincoln* (Albert and Charles Boni, 1930), p. 304; and Alexander L. George and Juliette L. George, *Woodrow Wilson and Colonel House: A Personality Study* (John Day, 1956), p. 320.

45. Richard E. Neustadt, *Presidential Power* (Wiley, 1960), p. 180.

feeling of awe about presidents."[46] Nor does presidential ambition describe a set of personality traits, given candidates as diverse as Eugene McCarthy and Lyndon Johnson.

Presidential ambition sets off a sort of biological clock. The Constitution requires that a president must be at least thirty-five years of age. Realistically candidates do not run much before their mid-forties or after their mid-sixties. With elections coming at four-year intervals, this allows five shots at the office. At least one chance must be deducted, though, because incumbents are almost always renominated. A Republican who reached the age of presidential ascent after the 1952 election, for example, would have had to stand aside in 1956 and 1972 while Presidents Eisenhower and Nixon ran for second terms. Thus presidential opportunity is more like a four-per-lifetime proposition. Yet the odds are even longer in that three unsuccessful races for the nomination turns a candidate into a laugh line for late-night TV comedians. Reagan escaped this fate by winning nomination on his third try. Indeed, the fact that sitting presidents were seriously challenged for renomination in 1968, 1976, and 1980 can be partly explained by how narrow is the window of opportunity for those with presidential ambition.

In short, contenders have remarkably little maneuvering room, and much of their strategic planning is held hostage to fortuity. Take the case of Richard Nixon who reached the White House in 1969 via this Rube Goldberg "stratagem": (a) run for president in 1960 against John Kennedy and lose by a hair; (b) seek a way to sit out the 1964 race so you can run in 1968 when Kennedy's second term ends; (c) decide to run for governor of California in 1962 so you can promise you will serve a four-year term; (d) lose the gubernatorial race, move to New York, and retire from seeking office; (e) watch the Republican party self-destruct in the 1964 election and the Democratic party self-destruct over the Vietnam War; (f) return from exile to be elected president in 1968.[47] Unlike the lower rungs on the political ladder, where aspirants

46. Jimmy Carter, *Why Not the Best?* (Broadman, 1975), p. 137.
47. See Jules Witcover, *The Resurrection of Richard Nixon* (Putnam, 1970), esp. pp. 25–35.

for an office have more time to wait for their most opportune moment (and may even be rewarded for being the good soldier, putting party above self), a person on the presidential track has little incentive to wait. To do so means that professional staff, volunteers, financial backers, and sympathetic political leaders will drift into other camps. A rule of thumb might be that each serious contender gets three chances and one bye. Robert Taft, for instance, sought the Republican nomination in 1940, 1948, and 1952, but passed in 1944. William Jennings Bryan was the Democratic nominee in 1896, 1900, and 1908, passed in 1904, and became increasingly implausible after his third defeat. Nor are there Damon-and-Pythias relationships in this hardball world. If a bunch of greats happen along in the same era, some will be pushed out of the way on the road to the White House. Thus are all persons with presidential ambition generationally trapped. Years from now we will be able to identify the politicians for whom 1988 was the year of the bye.

This formulation does not assume that all persons with presidential ambition will run for president, merely that persons without presidential ambition will not run for president and all persons who run for president have presidential ambition. Likewise, all professional politicians do not run for president, but all serious candidates for president are professional politicians—at least until the nation produces Ike-like heroes again. It is this combination of ambition and political professionalism that limits the field in any given election year. For example, Lowell Weicker, a liberal Republican senator, said in 1987 that he had presidential ambition but would not run for president in 1988. As a professional politician he knew that when his party was in a very conservative mood he "would stand no chance whatsoever . . . for getting the nomination. . . ."[48]

In our eternal search for the structural fix—Charles Krauthammer's felicitous phrase—there are modest ways to expand the

48. Quoted in Richard E. Cohen, "Weicker's Wing," *National Journal* (January 10, 1987), p. 108.

pool of presidential contenders in a particular presidential generation, such as by repealing the Twenty-second Amendment, revising gubernatorial election schedules, and revoking the constitutional ban against naturalized citizens serving as president. But under the Twenty-second Amendment, added to the Constitution in 1951, only three persons have been prevented from running for president—Dwight Eisenhower in 1960, Richard Nixon in 1976, and Ronald Reagan in 1988—and none of them would have sought the office again anyway.[49] An additional governor or two might be encouraged to seek the presidency if they did not have to give up their state job to make the race, but there are now only twelve states in which presidential and gubernatorial elections fall in the same year.[50] And while naturalized citizens (discriminated against under Article II, Section 4) deserve to be treated equally with the native-born, removal of this impediment would not result in a massive incursion of presidential hopefuls.[51] Another means of encouraging more

49. The history of amending the Constitution has almost always had the effect of expanding the rights of citizens (the Bill of Rights, the Reconstruction amendments following the Civil War, direct election of U.S. senators, female suffrage, presidential vote for the District of Columbia, abolition of the poll tax, and the eighteen-year-old vote). But the Twenty-second Amendment denies citizens the right to elect the same president more than twice consecutively. This is an idea that is bad in principle and works well in practice, presidents usually being of an age where eight years is a sufficient drain on their energies. Nevertheless, it should be up to the voters to decide. For arguments favoring retention, see Thomas E. Cronin, "Two Cheers for the 22nd Amendment," *Christian Science Monitor*, February 23, 1987.

50. The states that presently hold elections for governor and president in the same year are Delaware, Indiana, Missouri, Montana, North Carolina, North Dakota, Utah, Washington, West Virginia, New Hampshire, Rhode Island, and Vermont (the last four having two-year terms for governor).

51. Among the prominent naturalized citizens are foreign policy experts Henry Kissinger and Zbigniew Brzezinski, U.S. ambassador to Austria Henry A. Grunwald, industrialists An Wang and Gerald Tsai, journalists James Reston and Max Frankel, university president Hanna H. Gray, scientist Albert Sabin, scholar Kenneth Clark, Vermont Governor Madeleine Kunin, U.S. Senator Rudy Boschwitz, and U.S. Representatives Mervyn M. Dymally, Samuel Gejdenson, Ernest L. Konnyu, Thomas P. Lantos, and Ted Weiss. Persons born abroad whose parents are U.S. citizens are thought to be eligible to serve as president,

candidacies, some contend, would be to lower the cost of running for president.[52] Contemplating the next nomination fight, Edward J. Rollins, who headed President Reagan's 1984 campaign, said, "Anyone who isn't able to raise between $6 million and $8 million in 1987 is not going to be a player."[53] But while this is a great deal of money in terms of personal wealth, in commercial terms it means that the race for a presidential nomination has about the same price tag as a small fleet of New York City taxicabs (at $100,000 per medallion) or a midwestern newspaper of 10,000 to 12,000 circulation.

If fine-tuners wish to alter the type of persons who seek the presidency, the best place to tinker is the vice presidential selection process. For who gets the nod for vice president is the single most important predictor of future nominees for president. (Thirty percent of the men who have been major-party candidates for president since 1900 previously had been vice presidents or vice presidential candidates, 50 percent since 1960.) The presidential nominee's choice for vice president is usually a governor, senator, or House member—that is, another professional politician. The conventional wisdom is that a running mate can add electoral weight to the ticket; but in fact, John Kennedy may be the only president who owes his election to his choice for vice president, since Lyndon Johnson was the reason the Democrats carried Texas in 1960. When voters decide who will be the next president, the attributes (or lack thereof) of the vice presidential candidates are a very modest influence, suggesting that presidential conventions can afford to be a lot more daring if they desire to bring new blood into the political system, that is, if Americans prefer

---

although this has not been decided in the courts. See Edwin S. Corwin, *The Constitution and What It Means Today*, 14th ed. (Princeton, 1978), pp. 154–55.

52. For the counterargument that "we need to spend more, not less, on politics," see Tom Wicker, "Foreword," in Herbert E. Alexander, *Money in Politics* (Washington, D.C.: Public Affairs Press, 1972), p. vii.

53. Phil Gailey, "Babbitt of Arizona First Democrat to Form Key Presidential Group," *New York Times*, January 8, 1987.

to have their leaders come from outside the ranks of professional politicians. [54]

The fascination with process that has governed the energies of political science and political journalism has made academics increasingly useful to politicians and other practitioners, while at the same time journalists such as David S. Broder have added a new richness to the public understanding of politics. The matter of process has consequences for the presidential selection system, and the rapidity of change since 1968 has seemingly created a series of near-laboratory experiments. By changing the composition of the national convention can a party increase its chances of electoral success? In what proportions should parties use delegate slots to reward the faithful or encourage converts? Will an altered convention produce a different sort of platform? Which changes fuel ideology and which changes tamp it? Will presidents differently chosen become beholden to different groups and individuals? What changes increase voter participation? Has a decade of changes invigorated the parties or made them even less important in our society? All questions worth asking—and answering.

And yet in the paramount purpose of the parties' process— choosing the nominees to be president of the United States— which narrows the voters' choice from any native-born American of thirty-five years or older to two finalists, changes in the system since Lord Bryce's time do not limit the field of serious candidates or alter the character of the winners. While there are a few contenders who would not have previously emerged, such as Jesse Jackson and Pat Robertson, they have not yet been successful. There may also have been marginal or regional contenders of the past, such as Richard Russell of Georgia in 1952, who would not enter the race today. But in broad outline then and now, and with rare exceptions, these contenders for the nomination are professional politicians, people of extraordinary ambition who

54. For proposals on changing the way vice presidential nominees are selected, see pp. 35–36.

cannot be discouraged by changes in the rules of the game. This ambition determines the number who seek the presidency at any one time, taking into account the modest room for strategic maneuver. No doubt a particular contender will be more advantaged by one change in the process than will another, just as different contenders will be differently affected by the rate of employment and the rate of inflation. But those possessed by presidential ambition will participate regardless of whether selection occurs through a national primary, a series of regional primaries, a combination of state primaries and caucuses, or any permutation of the above.

Any democratic system is likely to produce the same range of contenders; in this regard, process does not determine outcome. A change in process may have some effect on which contender wins a specific nomination, and some presidential attributes are tested by the process. But regrettably for voters, journalists, social scientists, and students, the process will neither predict nor determine the chances of the winners' turning out to be great presidents.

Bibliography

THIS BIBLIOGRAPHY is designed for the reader who is delving into the topic of presidential selection for the first time. More specialized studies are cited in the footnotes that accompany this essay.

The Presidency

Bailey, Thomas A. *Presidential Greatness: The Image and the Man from George Washington to the Present.* Appleton-Century, 1966.

Barber, James David. *The Presidential Character: Predicting Performance in the White House.* Rev. ed. Prentice-Hall, 1977.

Corwin, Edward S. *The President: Office and Powers, 1787–1984.* Rev. ed. New York University Press, 1984.

Cronin, Thomas E. *The State of the Presidency.* Rev. ed. Little, Brown, 1980.

Cunliffe, Marcus. *The Presidency.* Rev. ed. Houghton Mifflin, 1987.

Donovan, Hedley. *Roosevelt to Reagan: A Reporter's Encounters with Nine Presidents.* Harper and Row, 1985.

Edwards, George C., and Stephen J. Wayne. *Presidential Leadership: Politics and Policy Making.* St. Martin's Press, 1985.

Grossman, Michael B., and Martha J. Kumar. *Portraying the President: The White House and the Media.* Johns Hopkins University Press, 1981.

Hargrove, Erwin C., and Michael Nelson. *Presidents, Politics, and Policy.* Johns Hopkins University Press, 1984.

Hodgson, Godfrey. *All Things to All Men: The False Promise of the Modern American Presidency.* Simon and Schuster, 1980.

Kellerman, Barbara. *The Political Presidency: The Practice of Leadership.* Oxford University Press, 1985.

Koenig, Louis W. *The Chief Executive.* Rev. ed. Harcourt, Brace and World, 1986.

Laski, Harold J. *The American Presidency: An Interpretation.* Harper, 1940.

Leuchtenburg, William E. *In the Shadow of FDR: From Harry Truman to Ronald Reagan.* Cornell University Press, 1983.

Lowi, Theodore J. *The Personal President: Power Invested, Promise Unfulfilled.* Cornell University Press, 1984.

Neustadt, Richard E. *Presidential Power.* Rev. ed. John Wiley, 1980.

Reedy, George. *The Twilight of the Presidency.* World, 1970.

Rossiter, Clinton. *The American Presidency.* Rev. ed. Harcourt, Brace and World, 1960.

Schlesinger, Arthur M., Jr. *The Imperial Presidency.* Houghton Mifflin, 1973.

Sorensen, Theodore C. *Decision-Making in the White House: The Olive Branch or the Arrows.* Columbia University Press, 1963.

Franklin D. Roosevelt

Burns, James MacGregor. *Roosevelt: The Lion and the Fox.* Harcourt, Brace and World, 1956.

———. *Roosevelt: The Soldier of Freedom.* Harcourt Brace Jovanovich, 1970.

Rosenman, Samuel I. *Working with Roosevelt.* Harper, 1952.

Schlesinger, Arthur M., Jr. *The Age of Roosevelt.* Vol. 1: *The Crisis of the Old Order.* Vol. 2: *The Coming of the New Deal.* Vol. 3: *The Politics of Upheaval.* Houghton Mifflin, 1957, 1958, 1960.

Sherwood, Robert E. *Roosevelt and Hopkins: An Intimate History.* Rev. ed. Harper, 1950.

Tugwell, Rexford G. *The Democratic Roosevelt.* Doubleday, 1957.

Harry S. Truman

Donovan, Robert J. *Conflict and Crisis: The Presidency of Harry S. Truman, 1945–1948.* Norton, 1977.

———. *Tumultuous Years: The Presidency of Harry S. Truman, 1949–1953.* Norton, 1982.

Miller, Merle. *Plain Speaking: An Oral Biography of Harry S. Truman.* Berkley, 1974.

Ferrell, Robert. *Harry Truman and the Modern American Presidency.* Little, Brown, 1983.

Truman, Harry S. *Memoirs.* Vol. 1: *Year of Decisions.* Vol. 2: *Years of Trial and Hope.* Doubleday, 1955, 1956.

Truman, Margaret. *Harry S. Truman.* Morrow, 1972.

Dwight D. Eisenhower

Adams, Sherman. *Firsthand Report: The Story of the Eisenhower Administration.* Harper, 1961.

Eisenhower, Dwight D. *The White House Years.* Vol. 1: *Mandate for Change, 1953–1956.* Vol. 2: *Waging Peace, 1956–1961.* Doubleday, 1963, 1965.

Greenstein, Fred I. *The Hidden-Hand Presidency: Eisenhower as Leader.* Basic Books, 1982.

Hughes, Emmet John. *The Ordeal of Power: A Political Memoir of the Eisenhower Years.* Atheneum, 1963.

Larson, Arthur. *Eisenhower: The President Nobody Knew.* Scribner's, 1968.

Parmet, Herbert S. *Eisenhower and the American Crusades.* Macmillan, 1972.

John F. Kennedy

Burns, James MacGregor. *John Kennedy: A Political Profile.* Harcourt, Brace, 1960.

Fairlie, Henry. *The Kennedy Promise: The Politics of Expectation.* Doubleday, 1973.

Parmet, Herbert S. *JFK: The Presidency of John F. Kennedy.* Dial, 1983.

Salinger, Pierre. *With Kennedy.* Doubleday, 1966.

Schlesinger, Arthur M., Jr. *A Thousand Days: John F. Kennedy in the White House.* Houghton Mifflin, 1965.

Sorensen, Theodore C. *Kennedy.* Harper and Row, 1965.

Lyndon B. Johnson

Dugger, Ronnie. *The Politician: The Life and Times of Lyndon Johnson.* Norton, 1982.

Evans, Rowland, and Robert Novak. *Lyndon B. Johnson: The Exercise of Power.* New American Library, 1966.

Goldman, Eric F. *The Tragedy of Lyndon Johnson.* Knopf, 1969.

Johnson, Lyndon B. *The Vantage Point: Perspectives of the Presidency, 1963–1969.* Holt, Rinehart and Winston, 1971.

Kearns, Doris. *Lyndon Johnson and the American Dream.* Harper and Row, 1976.

McPherson, Harry. *A Political Education.* Atlantic–Little, Brown, 1972.

Richard M. Nixon

Ambrose, Stephen E. *Nixon: The Education of a Politician, 1913–1962.* Simon and Schuster, 1987.

Brodie, Fawn M. *Richard Nixon: The Shaping of His Character.* Norton, 1981.

Evans, Rowland, and Robert Novak. *Nixon in the White House: The Frustration of Power.* Random House, 1971.

Mazo, Earl, and Stephen Hess. *Nixon: A Political Portrait.* Rev. ed. Harper and Row, 1969.

Nathan, Richard P. *The Administrative Presidency.* Rev. ed. John Wiley, 1983.

Nixon, Richard M. *The Memoirs of Richard Nixon.* Grosset and Dunlap, 1978.

Safire, William. *Before the Fall: An Inside View of the Pre-Watergate White House.* Doubleday, 1975.

Wills, Garry. *Nixon Agonistes: The Crisis of the Self-Made Man.* Houghton Mifflin, 1970.

Gerald R. Ford

Ford, Gerald R. *A Time to Heal: The Autobiography of Gerald R. Ford.* Harper and Row, 1979.

Nessen, Ron. *It Sure Looks Different From the Inside.* Simon and Schuster, 1978.

Reeves, Richard. *A Ford, Not a Lincoln.* Harcourt Brace Jovanovich, 1975.

terHorst, Jerald F. *Gerald Ford and the Future of the Presidency.* Third Press, 1974.

Jimmy Carter

Carter, Jimmy. *Keeping Faith: Memoirs of a President.* Bantam Books, 1982.

————. *Why Not the Best ?* Nashville, Tenn.: Broadman, 1975.

Glad, Betty. *Jimmy Carter: In Search of the Great White House.* Norton, 1980.

Powell, Jody. *The Other Side of the Story.* Morrow, 1984.

Shogan, Robert. *Promises to Keep: Carter's First Hundred Days.* Crowell, 1977.

Stroud, Kandy. *How Jimmy Won: The Victory Campaign from Plains to the White House.* Morrow, 1977.

Ronald Reagan

Barrett, Laurence I. *Gambling With History: Reagan in the White House.* Doubleday, 1983.

Cannon, Lou. *Reagan.* Putnam, 1982.

Dallek, Robert. *Ronald Reagan: The Politics of Symbolism.* Harvard University Press, 1984.

Edwards, Lee. *Ronald Reagan, A Political Biography.* Houston: Nordland, 1980.

The Presidential Campaign of 1956

Stevenson, Adlai E. *The New America.* Ed. by Seymour E. Harris. Harper, 1957.

Thomson, Charles A. H., and Frances M. Shattuck. *The 1956 Presidential Campaign.* Brookings, 1960.

The Presidential Campaign of 1960

David, Paul T., ed. *The Presidential Election and Transition, 1960–1961.* Brookings, 1961.

Kraus, Sidney, ed. *The Great Debates.* Gloucester, Mass.: Peter Smith, 1968.

Schlesinger, Arthur M., Jr. *Kennedy or Nixon: Does It Make Any Difference?* Macmillan, 1960.

White, Theodore H. *The Making of the President 1960.* Atheneum, 1961.

The Presidential Campaign of 1964

Cummings, Milton C., Jr., ed. *The National Election of 1964.* Brookings, 1966.

Gilder, George F., and Bruce K. Chapman. *The Party That Lost Its Head.* Knopf, 1966.

Hess, Karl. *In a Cause That Will Triumph: The Goldwater Campaign and the Future of Conservatism.* Doubleday, 1969.

Kessel, John H. *The Goldwater Coalition: Republican Strategies in 1964.* Bobbs-Merrill, 1968.

Shadegg, Stephen. *What Happened to Goldwater?* Holt, Rinehart and Winston, 1965.

White, Theodore H. *The Making of the President 1964.* Atheneum, 1965.

The Presidential Campaign of 1968

Chester, Lewis, Godfrey Hodgson, and Bruce Page. *An American Melodrama: The Presidential Campaign of 1968.* Viking, 1969.

McCarthy, Eugene J. *The Year of the People.* Doubleday, 1969.

McGinnis, Joe. *The Selling of the President 1968.* Trident, 1969.

Polsby, Nelson W. *The Citizen's Choice, Humphrey or Nixon.* Washington, D.C.: Public Affairs Press, 1968.

White, Theodore H. *The Making of the President 1968.* Atheneum, 1969.

The Presidential Campaign of 1972

Crouse, Timothy. *The Boys on the Bus.* Random House, 1973.
Dougherty, Richard. *Goodbye, Mr. Christian: A Personal Account of McGovern's Rise and Fall.* Doubleday, 1973.
May, Ernest R., and Janet Fraser, eds. *Campaign '72.* Harvard University Press, 1973.
Perry, James M. *Us & Them: How the Press Covered the 1972 Election.* Clarkson N. Potter, 1973.
Thompson, Hunter S. *Fear and Loathing: On the Campaign Trail '72.* Popular Library, 1973.
White, Theodore H. *The Making of the President 1972.* Atheneum, 1973.

The Presidential Campaign of 1976

Gold, Vic. *PR as in President.* Doubleday, 1977.
Moore, Jonathan, and Janet Fraser, eds. *Campaign for President: The Managers Look at '76.* Ballinger, 1977.
Reeves, Richard. *Convention.* Harcourt Brace Jovanovich, 1977.
Schram, Martin. *Running for President, 1976: The Carter Campaign.* Stein and Day, 1977.
Witcover, Jules. *Marathon: The Pursuit of the Presidency, 1972–1976.* Viking, 1977.

The Presidential Campaign of 1980

Bisnow, Mark. *Diary of a Dark Horse: The 1980 Anderson Presidential Campaign.* Southern Illinois University Press, 1983.
Drew, Elizabeth. *Portrait of an Election: The 1980 Presidential Campaign.* Simon and Schuster, 1981.
Germond, Jack W., and Jules Witcover. *Blue Smoke and Mirrors: How Reagan Won and Why Carter Lost the Election of 1980.* Viking, 1981.
Greenfield, Jeff. *The Real Campaign: How the Media Missed the Story of the 1980 Campaign.* Summit Books, 1982.
Moore, Jonathan. *The Campaign for President.* Ballinger, 1981.
Robinson, Michael J., and Margaret A. Sheehan. *Over the Wire and on TV: CBS and UPI in Campaign '80.* Basic Books, 1983.

The Presidential Campaign of 1984

Ferraro, Geraldine. *Ferraro, My Story*. Bantam Books, 1985.

Germond, Jack W., and Jules Witcover. *Wake Us When It's Over: Presidential Politics of 1984*. Macmillan, 1985.

Goldman, Peter, and Tony Fuller. *The Quest for the Presidency, 1984*. Bantam Books, 1985.

Henry, William, III. *Visions of America: How We Saw the 1984 Election*. Atlantic Monthly Press, 1985.

Moore, Jonathan, ed. *Campaign for President: The Managers Look at '84*. Dover, Mass.: Auburn House, 1986.

Shields, Mark. *On the Campaign Trail*. Chapel Hill, N.C.: Algonquin Books, 1985.

Index

☆ ☆ ☆ ☆ ☆ ☆ ☆ ☆ ☆ ☆ ☆ ☆ ☆ ☆ ☆ ☆ ☆